CREATIVE THINKING

Problem-Solving Skills and the Arts Orientation

Creativity Research

Mark A. Runco, Series Editor

Achieving Extraordinary Ends: An Essay on Creativity, by Sharon Bailin
Counseling Gifted and Talented Children, edited by Roberta M. Milgram
Creative Thinking: Problem-Solving Skills and the Arts Orientation, by
   John F. Wakefield
Divergent Thinking, by Mark A. Runco
More Ways Than One: Fostering Creativity, by Arthur J. Cropley
Perspectives on Creativity: The Biographical Method, by John E. Gedo and
   Mary M. Gedo

In Preparation:
Beyond Terman: Longitudinal Studies in Contemporary Gifted Education, edited by
   Karen Arnold and Rena Subotnick
Contexts of Creativity, by Leonora Cohen, Amit Goswami, Shawn Boles, and
   Richard Chaney
Creativity: Theories, Themes and Issues, by Mark A. Runco
Creativity and Affect, edited by Melvin Shaw and Klaus Hoppe
Creativity in Government, by Thomas Heinzen
Genius Revisited: High IQ Children Grown Up, by Rena Subotnik, Lee Kassan,
   Ellen Summers, and Alan Wasser
Nurturing and Developing Creativity: Emergence of a Discipline, Volume 2,
   edited by Scott G. Isaksen, Mary C. Murdock, Roger L. Firestien, and
   Donald J. Treffinger
Problem Finding, Problem Solving, and Creativity, edited by Mark A. Runco
Understanding and Recognizing Creativity: Emergence of a Discipline, Volume 1,
   edited by Scott G. Isaksen, Mary C. Murdock, Roger L. Firestien, and
   Donald J. Treffinger

CREATIVE THINKING

Problem-Solving Skills and the Arts Orientation

John F. Wakefield

University of North Alabama

ABLEX PUBLISHING CORPORATION
NORWOOD, NEW JERSEY

Copyright © 1992 by John F. Wakefield.

All rights reserved. No part of this publication may be reproduced, stored in a retrieval system, or transmitted, in any form or by any means, electronic, mechanical, photocopying, microfilming, recording, or otherwise, without permission of the author and publisher.

Printed in the United States of America

Library of Congress Cataloging-in-Publication Data

Wakefield, John F., 1952–
    Creative thinking : problem-solving skills and the arts orientation / John F. Wakefield.
       p.   cm.
    Includes bibliographical references and index.
    ISBN 0-89391-808-3
      1. Creative thinking.   2. Problem solving.   I. Title
LB1062.W28   1992

92-7306
CIP

Ablex Publishing Corporation
355 Chestnut St.
Norwood, NJ 07648

To Janelle, my wife
And Andrew, our son

Contents

List of Figures	*ix*
List of Tables	*xi*
PREFACE	*xiii*
CHAPTER 1. INTRODUCTION	1
Creativity and the Arts Orientation	2
A Measure of the Arts Orientation	3
The Arts Orientation and Cognition	5
Conclusion	11
CHAPTER 2. CREATIVE THINKING IN THE FIFTH GRADE	13
A Definition of Creative Thinking	13
The Kilby Study	14
Epilogue	25
CHAPTER 3. CLASSIFICATION OF COGNITIVE SKILLS	27
Closed Problems with Closed Solutions	28
Open Problems with Closed Solutions	30
Open Problems with Open Solutions	31
Closed Problems with Open Solutions	32
Uses of the Classification of Cognitive Skills	34
CHAPTER 4. CREATIVE THINKING AT AGE FOURTEEN	37
The Empirical Investigation	38
Implications	46
Conclusion	47
CHAPTER 5. CREATIVE THINKING OF HIGH SCHOOL SENIORS	49
The Empirical Investigation	51
Implications	58

CHAPTER 6. STORIES FOR THE THEMATIC APPERCEPTION TEST BLANK CARD	63
The Empirical Investigation	65
Discussion	77
CHAPTER 7. THEORETICAL AND EDUCATIONAL IMPLICATIONS	81
The Distribution of Creative Thinking	82
Creative Thinking and Conformity	86
Creative Thinking and Education	90
REFERENCES	95
APPENDIX A Occupations of Artistically Oriented Individuals	103
APPENDIX B Blank Card Stories by Fine Arts Majors	105
APPENDIX C Blank Card Stories with High Creativity Indices	111
AUTHOR INDEX	117
SUBJECT INDEX	121

List of Figures

2.1	Fifth-grade drawing ranked first in artistic merit by experts	21
3.1	Problem finding and solving situations	28
4.1	Shapes and lines for divergent-thinking exercises	40
4.2	Configuration of cognitive skills	43
5.1	Configuration of cognitive skills (revised)	54
6.1	Distribution of blank card response wordage for females	68
6.2	Average blank card response lengths for females by college	69
6.3	Average blank card response lengths for female LAS students by major	71
6.4	Distribution of blank card response wordage for males	72
6.5	Average blank card response lengths for males by college	73
7.1	Frequency distribution of creativity indices	83

List of Tables

1.1	Correspondences between personality types	4
2.1	Scale for rating drawings for artistic merit	17
2.2	Fifth-grade means and standard deviations	18
2.3	Intercorrelation of variables for fifth graders	19
4.1	Eighth-grade means and standard deviations	42
4.2	Intercorrelation of variables for eighth graders	44
4.3	Eighth-grade comparisons of arts-oriented students with other students	45
5.1	Correlations between career interests and creative behaviors	55
5.2	Correlations between career interests and cognitive skills	55
5.3	Correlations between cognitive skills and creative behaviors	56
5.4	Twelfth-grade comparisons of arts-oriented students with other students	57
6.1	Means and standard deviations for female college students	67
6.2	Creativity indices of female college students	71
6.3	Means and standard deviations for male college students	72
6.4	Means and standard deviations for fine arts majors	74
7.1	Cross-study comparisons of creative thinking	82
7.2	Comparisons of skew for untimed test scores	84
A.1	Artistically oriented individuals choosing artistic careers	104
A.2	Percentages of jobs and people	104

Preface

Studies of creative thinking and creativity tend to fall into one of two categories. On the one hand are case studies and research with small groups. These approaches offer the benefits of examining creative lives, examining the statements of creative individuals, or examining the creative products of a relatively small group of children or artists. Such studies offer significant insights into creative thinking that have interest in themselves and that suggest hypotheses for further testing. On the other hand are correlational or experimental designs that often involve larger groups and results that can be generalized to a relatively wide population. These studies tend to be confirmatory in nature, allowing one to test the limits of hypotheses and to explore educational implications. The smaller studies tend to appeal more to the artist, and the larger studies, to the scientist.

This book was written with the purpose of helping to bridge the gap between what I would call artistic and scientific studies of creative thinking. That gap exists not only as a fissure in creativity research, but as a form of self-estrangement, as if one must choose to be an artist or a scientist, a counselor or a researcher, a case study expert or a statistician. One must be a little of both in each dichotomy to read this book, which is written for the artist and scientist, the counselor and researcher, and the case expert and statistician interested in creative thinking. These different approaches actually create a productive tension, a far better relationship within the field of creativity research than the mutual alienation described by C.P. Snow (1963) in *The Two Cultures*.

This book does not attempt to present studies along the entire continuum, but to focus on analyzing the results from tests of individual subjects and research with groups of 70 or more. These studies should be accessible to both artists and scientists interested in creative thinking. Chapter 1 is a review of studies, both large and small, of the relation of cognitive skills to the arts. Chapters 2 and 6 may especially appeal to art educators or to career counselors who prefer to focus on the characteristics of talented individuals or small groups. Chapters 4 and 5, on the other hand, may appeal more to career development researchers or to cognitive psychologists who are accustomed to larger groups and multivariate statistics. Chapters 3 and 7 are somewhat speculative in nature and are written to be equally accessible to all.

A preference for the different methods of investigating creative thinking that the various chapters employ may lead the reader to skip portions of this book, but the reader is encouraged to work his or her way through all of the studies to develop a realistic way to think about creative thinking. Only by learning about a variety of approaches can we learn how to accept different approaches for the contribution to understanding that each has to offer and how to use multiple approaches in productive ways. Just as a stereoscopic perspective allows one to perceive in depth, studies from slightly different perspectives allow one to triangulate findings.

There is another pattern within this small volume. The studies proceed from an analysis of creative thinking of fifth graders, or children about 11 years old (Chapter 2), to eighth graders, or early adolescents about 14 (Chapter 4), to high school seniors, or youth about 18 (Chapter 5), to college students in their early 20s (Chapter 6). This organization permits one to view creative thinking progressively at different ages. Although the studies were not conceived as a developmental sequence, and thus lack the consistency of a deliberate cross-sectional design, the results lead in Chapter 7 to theoretical conclusions and to educational implications with considerable generality.

Earlier versions of the central chapters have appeared as refereed presentations or publications in diverse settings. The genesis of Chapter 2 was a presentation at the 1985 meeting of the Southeastern Psychological Association that became an article in *Child Study Journal.* Chapter 3 originated as a presentation at the National Topical Conference on the Future of Special Education sponsored in 1987 by the Council for Exceptional Children. Chapter 4 began as a presentation at the 1988 meeting of the American Educational Research Association. Chapter 5 was first presented at the 1989 meeting of the AERA and appeared in *Creativity Research Journal* later that year. Chapter 6 had its origins in a presentation to the Society for Personality Assessment in 1982 that became an article in the *Journal of Creative Behavior.* I would especially like to thank the editor of the *Creativity Research Journal,* Mark Runco, for permission to use a figure and several tables in this book that previously appeared in the *CRJ* article, and for conceiving of and editing the series of which this book is now a part.

No book can be written without the help of many others. Before the earliest study, R. Stewart Jones, late professor emeritus of educational psychology at the University of Illinois in Urbana-Champaign, was instrumental in developing my interest in creative thinking. He helped turn a casual observation about the TAT blank card into a dissertation. He is sorely missed.

Throughout the progress of the research and the writing, the administration of the University of North Alabama (UNA) has lent its support by funding multiple research proposals and supplemental requests. This support has been greatly appreciated. Elizabeth Walter, head of the art department at UNA, was kind enough to serve *gratis* as one of my judges of fifth graders' drawings. Dale Prediger, chief research scientist of the American College Testing Program, picked out my request to use the *ACT Interest Inventory* from "the stack" and graciously gave me permission to employ the UNIACT in two studies of the cognitive skills and vocational interests of secondary school students. David Pariser, associate professor of art education at Concordia University in Montreal, Canada, thoughtfully sent me the reference which begins Chapter 1.

Over the past 10 years, five research assistants—Joyce Caputo, Linda Docimo, Ann Eisenmenger, Janet Hudiburg, and Tom Satterfield—have done much of the testing and scoring, and all deserve my thanks for their conscientious efforts. In addition, almost a dozen teachers have let me or my assistants into their classrooms, often for several days, to conduct testing. In particular, I want to single out Mari Matteis, Advanced Placement English teacher at Coffee High School in Florence, Alabama, for opening doors for me to complete my study there.

Finally, I would like to thank two groups of students. My own students at the University of North Alabama participated in the development of some of the tests used in these studies. Their feedback improved early versions of these tests significantly. As for the hundreds of students from grade school through college who participated more directly in the research, I can say that without their patient and sometimes even eager cooperation, this book would never have been possible.

chapter 1
Introduction

When an artist starts out on a work of art, he has set himself some definite artistic problem that he is out to solve. He selects his characters, his time and his place, and then finds the particular and special circumstances which can allow the developments he desires to occur naturally, developing, so to say, without any violence on the artist's part in order to compel the desired issue, developing logically and naturally from the combination and interaction of the forces the artist has set into play. (Nabokov, 1981, p. 105)

In his lectures on Russian literature, Nabokov formulated what for creativity researchers has been an intriguing problem: the psychological relationship between the artist's thinking and the work of art. Many artists and philosophers have addressed this problem, but it may be slightly reformulated for a psychologist who wishes to work both with a wider group than professional artists, and within the boundaries of definitions that can be operationalized with accepted measures. A psychological rendition of this question might be, "What are the relationships between artistic interests, thinking skills, and behaviors?" From recent developments in theory and research, it may be expected that psychological constructs other than logic are involved in setting and solving an artistic problem (Wakefield, 1989).
    These elements seem to coexist with logic, and may well be bound to it through personality rather than through some cognitive construct, such as intelligence (MacKinnon, 1960). As Nabokov implied, these abilities may be complexly interrelated in their roles, or in terms of a more recent psychological formulation (Csikszentmihalyi & Getzels, 1988), problem-finding elements may exist in a metacognitive relation to logic. The concern of the psychologist is to sort out personality and cognitive variables in relation to one another and to the production components of the arts.

The task has proven to be difficult for a number of reasons. First, research on practicing artists has typically focused on just a few individuals. The results have great value for theory but need confirmation with larger numbers of individuals who may be less talented but who should exhibit some of the same interests, problem-solving skills, and behaviors as highly talented individuals. Second, there is no unified theory of creativity in psychology to serve as a point of departure. Research on creativity often seems to head in different directions without sustained attempts to understand the interrelationships between personality, cognition, and behavior. Yet some of the best research on creativity suggests that such relationships are crucial to understand what makes the person, the thought, and the product creative.

In this situation, I have chosen to study the *arts orientation* among children and youth. The studies described in the following chapters are intended to touch on points of theory to illustrate how they may have application to a larger number of individuals than previously thought. These empirical investigations build on the arts orientation as a clearly defined and widely accepted construct to explore its relationship to thinking skills and creative behaviors. These investigations are presented not as the end of a line of inquiry, but as a status report and a continuing program to suggest other studies. Too little is known about the phenomena explored here to pretend that these initial studies could be anything but exploratory.

CREATIVITY AND THE ARTS ORIENTATION

In the late 1950s, Holland introduced the concept of *adjustive orientations* as part of a theory of career choice. He said:

> Each orientation represents a somewhat distinctive life style which is characterized by preferred methods of dealing with daily problems, and includes such variables as values and "interests," preferences for playing various roles and avoiding others, interpersonal skills and other personal factors. For every person, the orientations may be ranked, according to their relative strengths, in a quasi-serial order or hierarchy. The life style heading the hierarchy determines the major direction of choice. (Holland, 1959, p. 36)

These orientations or lifestyles, which in theory led to vocational choice, were initially identified as motoric, intellectual, supportive, conforming, persuasive, and esthetic. Of particular interest to creativity researchers has been the esthetic orientation and the "methods of dealing with daily problems" that are correlated with it.

Eventually, these orientations were relabeled vocational personalities and arranged in a hexagon (Holland, 1985a). Clockwise on the hexagon these personality orientations were labeled Artistic (esthetic), Social (supportive), Enterprising (persuasive), Conventional (conforming), Realistic (motoric), and Investigative (intellectual). According to theory, the artistic person prefers artistic activities or occupations, uses artistic competencies to solve problems, perceives self as possessing certain characteristics (e.g., is expressive and original, and has artistic abilities), and values esthetic qualities. In particular, this type of individual prefers "ambiguous, free, and unsystematized activities" to those that are "explicit, systematic, and ordered" (Holland, 1985a, p. 20).

The relation of the arts orientation to creativity is evidenced through correlation with other indices of creativity. For example, as a part of their *NEO Personality Inventory,* Costa and McCrae (1985) developed an Openness scale to measure "toleration for and exploration of unfamiliar experiences" (p. 2). Characteristics of high scorers include creativity, as well as originality, imagination, broad interests, and a nontraditional outlook. When the Openness scale was recently correlated with the six orientations from Holland's *Self-Directed Search* (McCrae, 1987), it correlated strongly with the arts orientation, moderately with the investigative (scientific) orientation, and weakly with social and realistic orientations. These results provide evidence of the relation of the arts orientation to an independent index of creativity.

The validity of the arts orientation in terms of creative behaviors has been established through correlating the arts orientation with self-reports of creative behaviors—accomplishments in music, art, writing, and performing arts. In a large study, the Creative Arts scale of the *American College Testing Program Interest Inventory* (a measure of the arts orientation) correlated .3 on average with self-reports of creative behaviors (Lamb & Prediger, 1981, pp. 40–41). Correlations of five other ACT career interest scales with the self-reports were generally nonsignificant. In a smaller study reported in Chapter 5, Wakefield (1989) recently obtained similar results. As an index of creativity, the arts orientation appears to be better than any of the other five orientations, and the equal of other measures of creative personality.

A MEASURE OF THE ARTS ORIENTATION

The Creative Arts scale of the unisex edition of the *ACT Interest Inventory* (known as UNIACT) measures preference for "expressing oneself through activities such as painting, designing, singing, dancing, and writing," as well as "artistic appreciation of such activities" (Lamb & Prediger,

Table 1.1. Correspondences Between Personality Types

Holland (1959)	SDS Scales	UNIACT Scales
Esthetic	Artistic	Creative Arts
Supportive	Social	Social Service
Persuasive	Enterprising	Business Contact
Conforming	Conventional	Business Operations
Motoric	Realistic	Technical
Intellectual	Investigative	Science

1981, p. 1). The suggestion that esthetic appreciation (such as listening to music or reading literature) is an element of what the Creative Arts scale measures adds to its potential as a measure of the arts orientation because scores generally reflect esthetic values.

Correspondences between Holland types and UNIACT scales are portrayed in Table 1.1. Correlations between the corresponding portions of the SDS Artistic scale and the UNIACT Creative Arts scale are relatively high for both males and females (.62 and .61 over a six-week interval; Lamb & Prediger, 1981, p. 36). Correlations between the UNIACT Creative Arts scale and corresponding scales on other vocational interest instruments (such as the artistic scales on the *Kuder General Interest Survey* and the *Ohio Vocational Interest Survey*) are similarly high.

As a measure of the arts orientation, the UNIACT Creative Arts scale has several strengths. First, it is not a direct measure of accomplishment, although its correlations with experiences in the arts are relatively high. The scale permits one to assess the arts orientation apart from accomplishments, which may not yet be mature or may otherwise be difficult to identify. Accomplishments would not be appropriate, for example, in the case of a junior high school student, a more mature individual before a career adjustment or retirement, or an individual who may express artistic values in creative work, but not be employed in an artistic career.

Second, the UNIACT Creative Arts scale scores are sex-balanced, circumventing what some researchers regard as a persistent problem in interest assessment. Sex balance refers to the elimination of large sex differences in response to individual items; consequently, similar percentages of men and women might be considered to be artistic. Eleven percent of men and 16 percent of women in the UNIACT norms sample were classified with an arts orientation (Lamb & Prediger, 1981, p. 29). Many of these individuals do not initially enter artistic occupations, a development discussed in Appendix A.

Third, the ACT has established procedures for eliminating scores from consideration because of ambiguous interests. These procedures identify scores with excessive "like," "dislike," or "indifferent" responses and offer a control for insincerity or lack of selectivity. Such scores account for about 5 percent of the population, and reports inform the examinee that interests are not clear at this time. Information about scoring procedures is available from the ACT, along with norms down to the eighth grade.

Fourth, and perhaps most importantly, the UNIACT Creative Arts scale offers a theoretically clear and empirically validated approach to the measurement of the arts orientation. By fitting into a larger theory of personality orientations, it is conceptually clear. By approaching the arts orientation with established attributes of stability and validity, it has a solid psychometric foundation. Finally, by combining preferences for artistic activities and art appreciation, artistic interests are broad enough to apply to individuals who do not choose artistic careers, but who still may be artistic, and are narrow enough to distinguish artistic types from theoretically oppositional types of personality (e.g., conventional). By meeting the demands for theoretical clarity and empirical validity, the Creative Arts scale might be said to be a theoretically and technically sound measure of the arts orientation.

THE ARTS ORIENTATION AND COGNITION

The relationship between vocational interests and various measures of cognition goes back to the foundations of interest assessment. After reviewing the evidence in his classic *Vocational Interests of Men and Women*, E. K. Strong (1943) concluded that "occupational interest scales measure traits which are not primarily associated with intelligence" (p. 333). In reference to scales for men, he added that "men of high intelligence are more likely to have the interests of scientists, public accountants, lawyers, and writers and less likely to have the interests of men dealing with office procedures and with people—selling and serving them" (p. 334).

More recent research has not revealed a much different pattern of intelligence in relation to the UNIACT scales. Although one should be cautious when using the ACT Composite test score as a measure of general intelligence, the expected pattern holds up (Lamb & Prediger, 1981, pp. 40–41): ACT Composite scores for men and women correlate with interest in science (.36 and .29) followed by interest in the arts (.12 and .19). The ACT Composite score does not correlate positively with the other four interest scales, and in fact, for both men and women correlates slightly negatively with interest in conventional careers ($-.12$), as Strong (1943) might have expected. High school grade-point averages follow a similar but weaker pattern: They predict interest in science ($rs = .34$ and .23), but they do not predict interest in the arts or other vocational areas.

"Convergers" and "Divergers"

The findings are not more significant when intelligence is broken down into traditional components. Early efforts by Adkins and Kuder (1940) using Thurstone's (1938) *Tests for Primary Mental Abilities,* and more recent work by Kelso, Holland, and Gottfredson (1977) using the *Armed Forces Vocational Aptitude Battery* have generally not been successful in identifying other patterns of interest in relation to aptitudes. This line of inquiry might appear fruitless, if it were not for research begun by Hudson (1966, 1968) in England that has been pursued by several others. These reports have largely appeared in U.K. journals, resulting in a communications gap that may explain why this line of inquiry has generally not been pursued in the United States.

Hudson researched the thinking skills and curricular specialties of English school boys in what would correspond in America to their high school years. Hudson found that among intelligent boys, "it is those who are relatively good at free associating (the 'divergers') who are attracted towards the arts, while those who are relatively weak in this (the 'convergers') are drawn towards science and technology" (Hudson, 1987, p. 172). The coincidence of career interests with thinking skills has strong "implications for both the study of career choice and of originality" (Hudson, 1968, p. 1).

Hudson was referring to Guilford's (1956) distinction between convergent and divergent thinking. "Convergent production," Guilford noted, "is in the area of logical deductions or at least of compelling inferences" (1967, p. 171). Thought converges on a solution "when the input information is sufficient to determine a unique answer" (p. 171). Divergent production, on the other hand, involves the "generation of information from given information, where the emphasis is on variety and quantity of output from the same source; likely to involve transfer" (emphasis removed, p. 213). One means of summarizing the distinction between convergent and divergent thinking is that "in convergent production we are generating logical *necessities*" whereas "in divergent production we are generating logical *possibilities*" (p. 215).

Convergent-thinking skills have been commonly regarded as closely related to general intelligence, although representative correlations are hard to find, perhaps because of the redundancy. Divergent-thinking skills are evoked on very different kinds of exercises (e.g., listing different uses for a brick) and tend to correlate quite variably with IQ. Summarizing many studies, Torrance (1967) found the relationship between divergent thinking and IQ to average .06 for his figural and .21 for his verbal divergent-thinking measures. Looking over results from a wider range of divergent-thinking tests, Barron and Harrington (1981) concluded that .3 "is a reasonable estimate of central tendency" for these correlations, although they also seemed to be highly dependent on the type of divergent-thinking exercise, the heterogeneity of the sample, and the testing conditions.

In Hudson's research, convergent and divergent biases were not determined by levels of raw scores, but by score differences that involved subtracting one standardized score from another. Cognitive biases were measured only in relation to both scores; thus the emphasis on *relative* strengths of scores as opposed to differences between levels of raw scores, which other researchers found could not distinguish arts from science orientations (Haddon & Lytton, 1971; Nuttall, 1973).

Hudson attributed convergent-science and divergent-arts biases to differences in temperament or personality, focusing on defense mechanisms. The converger's defenses "protect him from controversy" and "limit the expression of his feelings," whereas the diverger has no such inhibition and is open to a wider range of feelings (1966, p. 89), even though the feelings might not run as deeply. In caricature, "the converger takes refuge from people in things; the diverger takes refuge from things in people" (1966, p. 91).

This dimension of personality fits neatly with recent developments in vocational theory that distinguish individuals according to two continua: ideas/data and things/people (Prediger, 1982). Although scientific and artistic orientations are similar with respect to their relation to ideas, they differ in their relations to things and people. Scientifically oriented individuals (Hudson's convergers) tend to express interest in things more than in people, whereas artistically oriented individuals (Hudson's divergers) tend to express interest in people more than in things.

Virtually all of the subsequent investigations of the convergent-science and divergent-arts biases confirmed Hudson's findings (for an exception, see Cropley, 1967), although some results complicated the picture. Early confirmation came with a study of high school students in Australia (Cropley & Field, 1968); studies of college students in Scotland (Mackay & Cameron, 1968), Australia (Field & Poole, 1970; Rump & Dunn, 1971), South Africa (Moerdyk, 1971), England (Child & Smithers, 1973), and the United States (Kirkland, 1974), and one longitudinal study in England (Povey, 1970). In the late 1960s and early 1970s, researchers distinguished convergent-science and divergent-arts biases on a fairly consistent basis.

Other reports in part confirmed the findings but also posed alternative explanations. Smithers and Child (1974), for example, rejected different forms of neuroticism as the cause for the convergent-science and divergent-arts biases. Yčas and Pascal (1974) suggested that the biases are mislabeled, and should more accurately be "convergent-science" and "divergent-esthetic." Lloyd-Bostock (1979) found that the verbal bias of verbal divergent-thinking test scores might explain their relation to the arts orientation, and the biases might more accurately be labeled "nonverbal-science" and "verbal-arts."

Perhaps the most poignant criticism came from Lloyd-Bostock (1979). Working with intelligence test scores with separable verbal/numeric and diagrammatic components, scores on one figural and two verbal divergent-thinking tests, and expressed choices of different school subjects, she conducted a factor analysis of the results of testing 310 14-year-old boys and girls. She found the factor structure to distinguish divergent thinking from intelligence, but both factors were predominantly verbal, neither explaining variances on the figural tests (of diagrammatic intelligence and divergent thinking). She concluded that intelligence is correlated with both arts and science orientations, as Hudson had clearly implied, and that divergent thinking is correlated with an arts orientation, but that the failure of divergent thinking to correlate with the science orientation was a result of verbal and nonverbal test biases, and not the degree to which tests were open-ended.

Test bias is an important issue and to some extent separable from the issue of cognitive bias. Test bias is more easily detected when one correlates raw scores than scores derived through subtraction. Raw score correlations have not typically been used in this line of research, except in McCrae's (1987) work. Although Rump (1982) appears to have preceded McCrae in correlating arts interest with divergent thinking, McCrae appears to have been the first to have correlated a set of vocational personality measures with multiple measures of divergent thinking (all verbal). Divergent thinking correlated about equally with the arts and science orientations (.27 and .24). What appears to be more significant was that divergent thinking correlated with both of these orientations more highly than with enterprising, conventional, and realistic orientations. Although McCrae's results did not confirm or disconfirm Hudson's findings, they supported the conclusion that divergent thinking correlates with interest in the arts. They do not resolve the issue of whether or not this relationship reflects a verbal test bias, but they do suggest that whatever accounts for the relationship has implications beyond arts and science.

Thus far two cognitive skills seem to relate to the arts orientation: convergent and divergent thinking. Scoring techniques to determine bias or the exclusion of groups high in overlapping scores ("all-rounders") may account for the consistency of findings, but placed in a wider perspective, these biases are not the lingering issue, at least as far as this review is concerned. A more relevant concern is whether or not a verbal test bias is sufficient to explain the correlation between divergent thinking and the arts orientation. This question is addressed in Chapter 2.

Problem Finding

The earliest statement on problem finding, as opposed to problem solving, might be attributed to Paul Souriau (1881) writing about the faculty of *invention: Il y a quelque chose de méchanique pour ainsi dire dans l'art de trouver les solutions. L'esprit vraiment original est celui qui trouve les problèmes* ["There is something mechanical, as it were, in the art of finding solutions. The truly original mind is that which finds problems"] (p. 17). Statements by Albert Einstein (Einstein & Infeld, 1938, p. 95) in science and Henry Moore (1985, p. 72) in art suggest that problem-finding skills or abilities might be quite distinct from skills or abilities useful in problem solving.

The first study of problem finding by artists was done by Getzels and Csikszentmihalyi (1967, 1976) with visual arts students at the Art Institute of Chicago. Getzels and Csikszentmihalyi tested visual arts students with a variety of measures (including verbal divergent-thinking tests), and then set up a problem situation in which students were asked to select from an array of objects those which would be useful for an experimental drawing that each would make. Although scores on intelligence and other cognitive measures did not distinguish this group from college norms, scores on personality and values measures did. One of the early and more striking findings was the similarity of art students to research scientists and architects in their imaginativeness and esthetic values (Getzels & Csikszentmihalyi, 1967).

Expert ratings of the students' final drawings for esthetic value and originality (but not craftsmanship) correlated highly with problem-finding variables during the problem formulation stage (i.e., the number of objects manipulated, the unusualness of objects manipulated, and the intensity of object exploration) as well as problem-finding variables scored from an interview. In their seven-year follow-up of fine arts students, Getzels and Csikszentmihalyi (1976) found that success as an artist was significantly correlated with a problem-finding composite score. The 1981 follow-up of fine artists in midlife (Csikszentmihalyi & Getzels, 1988) suggested that recognition and income as an artist could still be predicted from intensity of object exploration and expressed concern with problem finding measured in 1963.

What is not as clear is the relation of these findings to previously reviewed research. Although convergent-thinking tests were not found to distinguish art students from the general college population, that population is itself attenuated by the general exclusion of students in the lower IQ ranges, who in disproportionate numbers do not graduate from high school, or, if they do, choose not to go to college. Whereas the average IQ for the total population is 100, that for high school graduates has been estimated at 105, and that for college graduates, 115 (Matarazzo,

1972, p. 178). And whereas a fairly significant percentage of individuals with below average IQs finish high school, far fewer seem to have entered college, at least at the time that data were collected for the norms (Matarazzo, 1972, p. 283). IQ test norms for college in the past, then, have represented a sample that was average and above in relation to the general population. The sample of arts students in the Chicago study appears to have been a sample of capable convergent thinkers.

More difficult to explain is the failure of the divergent-thinking test scores to differ from the college norms. There are a few clues. First, scores of both male and female visual arts students were significantly above average on a test of spatial visualization (Getzels & Csikszentmihalyi, 1976, p. 253). The visual talents of the group seem to be reflected in these test scores. Second, all of the divergent-thinking tests administered in the study were verbal. From a study of a large number of children who took batteries of both IQ and divergent-thinking tests in their teens (Magnusson & Backteman, 1978), it may be concluded that spatial abilities correlate positively but very weakly with verbal divergent thinking (.17 for males and .25 for females). Somewhat surprisingly, the correlation between spatial abilities and figural divergent-thinking tests may even be lower (.09 and .20 in this study). Verbal divergent-thinking test scores did not reflect the visual talents of the visual artists, but test selection was not to blame for the absence of this correlation.

Partial replications of the Chicago study with younger subjects have only appeared in the last few years. Michael Moore (1985), for example, identified eight high-creative middle-school students using a personality measure (Davis & Rimm, 1982), and ratings by a teacher and an administrator. He matched them with eight low-creative students in terms of sex, grade, and IQ. Students were individually asked to select objects from an array for a theme that each student would write about the objects. Even with this small group, differences between high-creative and low-creative groups were significant for two of three problem-finding variables during problem formulation (number and uniqueness of objects touched). Differences were also significant in degree of symbolic transformation of objects, length of essays (fluency), and judgments by teachers of originality and esthetic value, but not of craftsmanship. This study extended the conclusions of Getzels and Csikszentmihalyi (1976) about the thought processes of developing fine artists to intelligent and creative children in middle school language arts. Creative production seemed to call for concern about problem finding.

A second partial replication was recently reported by Scott (1988). Her purpose was to discover the personality characteristics that distinguished artistically talented students from other groups in 11th and 12th grade. Using three groups (artistic, academic, and average) of over 100 students each, and some of the same personality measures as used in the Getzels and Csikszentmihalyi study, she found the artistic group to be less sociable and more radical than the academic and average groups; less intelligent, trusting, and assured than the academic group; and more self-sufficient and relaxed than the average group. The findings of less sociability, more radicalism, and greater self-sufficiency than average replicate those of the Chicago study. Other findings by Scott were higher esthetic values, and lower economic values than average and academically talented students, which also replicated earlier findings.

Although Scott's (1988) research did not raise the subject of cognitive skills directly, her findings regarding intelligence closely paralleled those of the Chicago study and added biographical information of interest. Artistically talented 11th and 12th graders scored the same as art students in the Chicago study on the measure of intelligence used in both studies (Factor B of the *16PF Questionnaire*). The high school students might be said to have average and above intelligence in relation to the general population. On a biographical questionnaire, they appear in many ways average in comparison to the academically oriented group: They are less likely to receive very high grades, to try harder to achieve than others, and to plan to attend college. More often than the other groups of students, however, they report art an important high school class and an acceptable career for them in the eyes of their parents.

CONCLUSION

The arts orientation, as defined by interest in artistic activities and esthetic appreciation, seems to be related to several cognitive skills or abilities. These skills and abilities appear useful in artistic problem solving but may not be closely related among themselves. They seem to include convergent thinking, which is a form of logical deduction, and divergent thinking, which generates logical possibilities. They also seem to include a group of skills or abilities which may collectively be labeled "problem finding." Problem-finding abilities may involve more than cognition, including conative and affective elements.

What this review of the literature on the arts orientation and cognitive skills reveals is a loosely drawn pattern of cognitive skills in relation to the arts orientation, extending from junior high school through college and beyond. These relationships seem to have a pattern that varies somewhat with the theoretical perspective of the viewer and the selection of the sample, but is not amorphous. What the research seems to call for is a precise definition of the relationships through hypothesis formulation, selection or design of specific tests of cognitive skill, and their use with groups over a range of ages to test the relationships between problem-solving skills and the arts orientation.

chapter 2
Creative Thinking in the Fifth Grade

There are two reasons why a formal definition of creative thinking has awaited the review of research on problem-solving skills and the arts orientation. First, the definition that will be offered evolved out of such research and relies on it for a background. Second, this definition is necessary to comprehend the designs of investigations pursued in this and later chapters. The literature review, then, serves as a necessary antecedent to the definition of creative thinking and as an introduction to the following chapters.

A DEFINITION OF CREATIVE THINKING

The definition of creative thinking is derived from research on open-ended problem solving—such as divergent thinking—and research on problem finding. Guilford (1975) said that divergent-thinking exercises differed from convergent exercises in "the degree of restraint or limitation upon the desired answer" (p. 40). Similarly, problem finding has been said to differ from problem solving in the degree to which the problem has a known formulation (Dillon, 1982; Getzels, 1975; Getzels & Csikszentmihalyi, 1976). If these two conditions are coordinated and combined, they suggest a problem situation that constrains neither problem formulation nor problem solution. Creative thinking may be defined as *a meaningful response to any situation which calls for finding a problem and solving it in one's own way.*

It is difficult to imagine a situation in which there are constraints neither on the problem nor on its solution. The type of problem to be formulated offers a form of constraint, such as the logical form of divergent thinking investigated by Guilford and Torrance, or the Piagetian mode of problem finding investigated by Arlin (1975, 1977). In practice, another constraint may be ontological, given that knowledge can only progress with respect to what is known. Added constraints may be esthetic, both in science and the arts. Still, problems may be classified in relation to the various situaitons that they pose the problem solver (e.g., Getzels, 1975). My own analysis of the various possibilities will be elaborated in Chapter 3. At this point, it is sufficient to note that problems are defined and solved in different contexts. These contexts restrict the freedom of the problem solver to differing degrees.

THE KILBY STUDY

This conception of problem finding and solving suggests that a potentially very fruitful, but virtually unexplored territory for research is the systematic alteration of problems to introduce greater or lesser degrees of constraint. Theory is surprisingly well developed in comparison to empirical research in this area. Studies have focused on what in retrospect appear to be relatively minor alterations, such as whether or not open-ended tests should be timed (e.g., Hattie, 1977, 1980). As Wallach (1985) noted in a review of this research, timing really seems to make little difference. Whether or not more substantive alterations make any difference is an unasked question, but developments in theory suggest that it is a significant question, and it is the question that motivated the empirical research presented in this and other chapters.

As Arlin's (1975) study implies, however, problem-solving skills of a given type must developmentally precede the ability to find or set that type of problem. The implication for children who are 10 and 11 years of age is that the type of problem that they can effectively formulate is not logical in either Piaget's formal or concrete sense, but must be prelogical, that is, both found and solved by preoperational thinking skills. If one wishes to begin a study of problem *finding* with children in the fifth grade, then, one should not expect adultlike creative thinking. Instead, one should begin with problem-solving tasks that do not call for mature logic.

Such tasks exist in some of the open-ended exercises designed by Wallach and Kogan (1965) to test the divergent thinking of fifth graders. These tasks call for the subject to supply multiple meanings or interpretations for each of a series of lines or patterns drawn on four-by-six inch cards. This task calls for associative but not necessarily logical thinking. To induce problem finding in this exercise, one may alter the problem situations posed in each series by introducing a blank card, then asking the child to draw his or her own pattern or line before interpreting it in as many ways as possible. This modification permits the child freedom to find a problem and solve it in his or her own way, but it does not call for logical thinking, either in problem-finding or problem-solution stages.

What the task seems to call for in the problem-finding stage is intuition. Intuition has been theorized as one element in problem finding (Getzels & Csikszentmihalyi, 1967; Wakefield, 1988) and is thought to be common among creative people in general (MacKinnon, 1978, pp. 130-131). "Intuitive perception" is the term MacKinnon coined in the late 1950s to describe perception that was not stimulus-bound (known as "sense perception"), but stimulus-free. Obviously, perception bound to the stimulus of a blank card would be bound to nothing at all.

By inserting a blank card among cards from each series, an experimenter can provide subjects with opportunities to find problems before solving them in a meaningful and individual way. Wakefield (1985) hypothesized that fluency of responses to such "creative" opportunities would correlate more highly with other measures of creativity than would fluency of responses to presented patterns and lines.

Method

Kilby School is the last laboratory school in the State of Alabama and is an administrative unit of the University of North Alabama. In 1984, the 23 pupils in the fifth grade (11 boys and 12 girls) were all tested with the modified divergent-thinking measures for a study of problem finding in a divergent-thinking exercise. Kilby has a fairly selective admissions policy, and the subjects' fourth-grade scores on a test of academic aptitude ranged from the 48th to the 99th percentile. On the *California Achievement Tests,* which were administered in the fifth grade the same month as the study measures, 17 pupils (74%) scored one year or more above the national mean grade placement. None scored one or more years below the mean. By all measures of scholastic ability and achievement, the group tested was above average, ranging from average to academically gifted.

This sample was judged especially appropriate for testing because of the "threshold hypothesis." This hypothesis asserts that creativity and intelligence are not closely related when subjects tested are average and above in ability. The threshold itself varies with the test, but there seems to be general agreement that subjects significantly below average do not possess the intellectual skills to be creative in any field (cf. Csikszentmihalyi & Getzels, 1988). Still, the threshold may be "surprisingly low" (MacKinnon, 1978, p. 123). By restricting the intellectual range of the sample to average and above, one can minimize the degree of autocorrelation that otherwise seems to result from correlating measures of creative thinking with intelligence.

Measures and Procedure. Cards 1 through 5 in both Pattern and Line Meanings were used as indicated in Wallach and Kogan's (1965) study, but subjects were presented with a blank card and a pencil after Card 4 in each series. The examiners gave these special instructions: "Here is a blank card and a pencil. Make a pattern (or line) of your own, then tell me all the different things it could be." Only mutually exclusive responses were accepted. Each pupil received two scores, one for divergent fluency and the other for creative thinking. The reliability of scores was estimated by correlating corresponding scores for Pattern Meanings with those for Line Meanings. These correlations, when adjusted by the Spearman-Brown prophecy formula, yielded reliability coefficients of .94 for divergent fluency and .82 for creative thinking. The diminished reliability of the creative-thinking score was interpreted as a function of estimating reliability over 2 items instead of 10.

Pattern and Line Meanings were followed by three subtests of the WISC-R, all of which were administered as in the Wallach and Kogan study. The three subtests were: Vocabulary (a verbal measure that correlates highly with the total battery score), Block Design (a measure of nonverbal intelligence that correlates highly with the total battery score and that calls for analytical thinking), and Picture Arrangement (a performance measure that relates to ability to see a situation whole and comprehend it). Scale scores were computed for each of these subtests.

Two other tests were administered to the group: the *Group Inventory for Finding Creative Talent,* or GIFT (Rimm, 1980) and the *California Achievement Tests* (as part of a routine assessment of progress). The GIFT yields three scale scores (Imagination, Independence, and Many Interests) and a total score. Total scores for the upper elementary level (Grades 5 and 6) seem adequately reliable for identification of individual talent and have been validated through correlation with ratings of drawings and stories for artistic merit (e.g., Davis & Rimm, 1977). According to the score report, eight of the Kilby students scored highly enough on the total score to indicate that "the child has characteristics similar to those of highly creative children." Normal curve equivalent scores were used on this test.

The *California Achievement Tests* were used in their 1977 edition. Scale scores were available for all students on language (mechanics and expression) and mathematics (computation and application) portions of the tests. Scores were also available for 22 students on the reading and spelling sections and on the total battery. For comparative purposes, the study used only the scores on the language and mathematics portions of the test battery.

Table 2.1. Scale for Rating Drawings for Artistic Merit*

Category	Description
5	Picture shows originality of idea and special talent in expression of idea.
4	Picture shows definite originality of idea, although expression of the idea may not show special talent.
3	Picture is not necessarily original, but slightly different from child's everyday life. It clearly shows an effort to create something more original, although the work may actually be similar in idea to other classmates' work.
2	Picture unoriginal or clearly copied from coloring book. An unusual detail or slightly more artistic attempt separates these from the first rating.
1	Picture very simple and unoriginal. Refers to child's everyday life. Plainest of pictures are included in this category. Expression of ideas is poor.

*After Rimm, S., & Davis, G. A. (1980). Five years of international research with GIFT: An instrument for the identification of creativity. *Journal of Creative Behavior, 14,* 35-46. Reprinted by permission.

Students were also given an opportunity to "draw a picture appropriate to the title, 'Playing Tag in the School Yard.' You may draw any picture you like—whatever you may imagine for this theme." This open-ended exercise (with no time limit) was adopted from the Getzels and Jackson (1962, p. 257) study of creativity and intelligence. Two raters (the head of the university art department and a graduate art student) were asked to rate the drawings for artistic merit on a scale from 1 to 5, as described in Table 2.1. The elements of artistic merit were perceived to be the originality of the idea and the degree of talent with which the idea was expressed (Rimm & Davis, 1980). Combined ratings (with a reliability of .77) and Spearman rank-order correlations were used in further computations with this variable.

Finally, students took the *ACT Interest Inventory* one year and three years later. Students initially took the UNIACT in its computerized form (called DISCOVER) at the university library, and 19 of the original 23 (83%) received stanines which could be used in later computations. Because the reliability and validity of the UNIACT is not established for this age level, only the Creative Arts scale was used in further calculations. The reliability of this scale was estimated (from the scores of eight pupils who volunteered to retake the inventory) to be .54. In the three-year follow-up, 18 students returned the mailed inventory in its regular form. All of these scores were usable, and raw scores were converted into stanines through norms for Grades 8-10 supplied by the ACT.

Two female research assistants were trained to administer individually the modified divergent-thinking exercises and the intelligence measures, but neither they nor the classroom teacher nor the raters of artwork were informed of the central hypothesis of the study. Each of the two research assistants tested approximately the same number of boys and girls. The

Table 2.2. Fifth-Grade Means and Standard Deviations ($N=23$)

Variable	Mean	SD
WISC-R Scales		
Vocabulary	12.9	2.5
Block Design	11.4	2.4
Picture Arrangement	11.3	1.9
Achievement Scales		
CAT Language	591.5	59.9
CAT Mathematics	507.4	39.0
Divergent Thinking	3.7	1.7
Creative Thinking	4.8	2.7
GIFT Total (NCE score)	60.0	17.6

group achievement and creativity measures were administered by the classroom teacher. The drawing exercise was completed after the pupils were finished with the group creativity measure. All of the initial testing (including the achievement testing) took place within two weeks.

A year later, when these 23 students were in the sixth grade, they completed a unit on vocational awareness (at the request of the researcher) by taking the UNIACT in its computerized form. Then three years after the initial testing, UNIACT surveys were mailed to the 23 original subjects. In a final follow-up effort six years after the initial testing, parents of the two students whose drawings were rated most highly in fifth grade were contacted about their child's artistic achievements through junior year in high school.

Results

The means and standard deviations of study variables are reported in Table 2.2. The WISC-R and CAT scores tended to be above average, especially in the domain of verbal ability and skills. Similarly, normal curve equivalent scores for the GIFT (which have an average of 50.0) were above average for this group, indicating characteristics related to creativity.

The intercorrelations of the variables are reported in Table 2.3. The central hypothesis was confirmed by the significant correlation (.46, $p < .05$) of the creative-thinking score (fluency of response to the personally drawn pattern and line) with the GIFT score, but a weaker correlation (.33, n.s.) of the divergent-thinking score with the GIFT score, despite the higher reliability of the divergent-thinking than the creative-thinking measure.

Results not presented in the table were correlations of creative and divergent thinking with subscales on the GIFT. Creative- and divergent-

Table 2.3. Intercorrelation of Variables for Fifth Graders ($N=23$)

	1. WISCV	2. WISCB	3. WISCP	4. CATL	5. CATM	6. DT	7. CT	8. GIFT	9.[a] ArtR	10[b] ArtI
1.	—	.66**	.37*	.34	.29	.45*	.23	.40*	−.23	.09
2.		—	.26	.49*	.28	.36*	.20	.31	−.03	.13
3.			—	.26	.38*	.18	.09	.26	−.06	.05
4.				—	.69**	.39*	.41*	.27	.05	.22
5.					—	.28	.40*	.41*	−.04	.20
6.						—	.76**	.33	.10	.36
7.							—	.46*	.38*	.43*
8.								—	.20	.40*
9.										.59**

Note: WISCV = WISC-R Vocabulary; WISCB = WISC-R Block Design; WISCP = WISC-R Picture Arrangement; CATL = CAT Language; CATM = CAT Math; DT = Divergent Thinking; CT = Creative Thinking; GIFT = *Group Inventory for Finding Creative Talent*; ArtR = Rated artistic merit of drawings; ArtI— = Artistic Interests.
[a] Spearman rank-order correlation coefficients
[b] $N = 19$
*$p < .05$
**$p < .01$

thinking scores correlated equally significantly with GIFT scores on scales for Imagination and Independence, but unequally with the scale labeled Many Interests. Although neither creative nor divergent thinking correlated significantly with Many Interests, the difference in correlations (.20 versus −.10) was statistically significant ($t = 2.09$, $p < .05$), that is, creative thinking correlated significantly more highly with Many Interests than did divergent thinking.

The difference in the concurrent validity of creative- versus divergent-thinking scores was more strikingly revealed with respect to the experts' ratings of drawings for artistic merit (shown in Table 2.3). Creative thinking significantly (.38, $p < .05$) predicted these ratings, whereas divergent thinking did not (.10, n.s.). This difference was perhaps related to the fact that unlike creative thinking and the ratings of drawings, divergent thinking was significantly correlated with both verbal and nonverbal intelligence (.45 and .36, $p < .05$).

Perhaps the most dramatic finding of the initial study was that, of all the measures, only creative thinking correlated significantly with the experts' ratings of drawings for artistic merit. In other words, these ratings were not correlated with intelligence or school achievement as measured in a traditional or routine manner.

Three measures in the initial study significantly predicted arts interest one year later. A highly significant correlation (.59, $p < .01$) was obtained between ratings of drawings for artistic merit and arts interest, which confirmed the validity of the ratings. Significant correlations were also obtained between arts interest and both creative thinking (.43, $p < .05$) and GIFT scores (.40, $p < .05$), confirming the predictions made through these scores. Arts interest may also have been predicted by divergent thinking (.36, n.s.) had a larger group of subjects returned usable scores.

To provide some follow-up information for these students in eighth grade, UNIACT surveys were sent out three years after the initial study to all of the original subjects who could be contacted by phone. Eighteen surveys (78% of the original sample) were returned. What was somewhat surprising was that none of the psychometric measures administered three years earlier predicted interest in the arts in eighth grade. Only rating of drawings for artistic merit significantly predicted arts interest three years later ($r = .45$, $p < .05$). Even fifth-grade arts interest fell short of correlating significantly with eighth-grade arts interest ($N = 15$, .33, n.s.). Artistic competence in the fifth grade emerged as the best predictor of an arts orientation in the eighth grade.

Although the statistical results of the three-year follow-up did not justify sending out surveys in high school to this group, parents of two of the students whose drawings were rated most highly were contacted about the achievements of their children by 11th grade. These data provided information for the following cases.

Case 1. The student ("Nicole") whose drawing was given the highest rating by art experts for artistic merit had average diverent- and creative-thinking scores in fifth grade. Her normal curve equivalent score on the GIFT was above average, but it did not reach the criterion for giftedness on this measure (the 85th percentile). A year after the initial testing, however, Nicole's "high-point" interests were technical or artistic careers, both with stainines of 9. By eighth grade, her interest in scientific careers was her high-point score (stanine 9), and interests in arts and enterprising careers were tied for second (stanine 8).

Nicole's talent and changes in interest are reflected in her training and development. After elementary school, she began attending a private, religiously oriented school with national recognition for academic excellence, but because of its small size and limited resources, without formal art or creative writing programs. From sixth to eighth grade, she received private art lessons, but unfortunately, this small art studio closed. Nicole is doing very well in high school with a "straight-A" average in her junior year, and she is making plans to go to college with an initial major in marine biology. Her parents indicated that she continues to enjoy art as a hobby.

According to the art experts, Nicole's drawing revealed some special features indicative of a special talent in art. Her drawing is reproduced in Figure 2.1. Of special interest to the experts was the central "chase." They noted that in contrast to most of the drawings, this one portrayed a

Figure 2.1. Fifth-grade drawing ranked first in artistic merit by experts.

girl chasing a boy. This portrayal was unusual, but their attention was also drawn to the expression in the eye of the boy being chased. The delight and excitement communicated by that glance over his shoulder! If the rating had been an art contest, this drawing would have been the winner. The second-place drawing was craftsmanlike, with more realistic figures, but according to the experts, did not reveal the same degree of talent in this domain.

Case 2. The student ("Sheha") whose drawing was rated second most highly for artistic merit ranked fourth in divergent thinking and second in creative thinking. Sheha was among those who scored highly enough on the GIFT to indicate that they possess characteristics of highly creative children. A year after initial testing, her high-point interest was in science (stanine of 9), followed by the arts (stanine of 8). By eighth grade, however, her interest in science had declined and had been surpassed by interests in the arts (still stanine 8) and social service careers (stanine 7).

Sheha's parents are both school teachers, and academic achievement is very important to them. Sheha has done very well in a large public high school, and by 11th grade was in all advanced placement (AP) classes. Although the high school has art and creative writing programs, her parents stressed Sheha's achievements in math and public speaking competitions. An essay she wrote about her family's way of celebrating a holiday tradition won an award from the local newspaper and was published. Although her parents have great interest in her entrance into a good college and indicated that math was her favorite subject, they did not indicate her likely major. Given Sheha's changes in interest in the past, one might infer that she may still be undecided about an initial college major.

Insights

Studies with small numbers of subjects can be criticized on the grounds that they are not representative of larger groups, or that results do not reflect small, but statistically significant relationships, but they also deserve to be defended on the same grounds. In a study of creative thinking and the arts orientation, intensive examination may yield as many insights as a more extensive study. The Kilby study was an attempt to study a classroom group intensively, using 10 carefully selected measures and repeated follow-ups to determine which results, if any, might have substantive as well as statistical significance.

The results indicated quite clearly that the psychometric measures used in this study did not have great power to predict an arts orientation over the long term. The experimental measure that operationalized the definition of creative thinking did predict artistic interests and ratings of drawings for artistic merit, but three years later, these ratings proved better predictors of artistic interests than did the measure of creative thinking. The first insight gained from this study is that *expert ratings of drawings (or stories) for artistic merit offer a means to identify artistic talent in elementary school that is superior to most if not all measures of cognitive skill or ability.* The cognitive measures used in this study could not match the judgment of experts, who in ordinary evaluations can function as consultants as well as raters.

One should hasten to add that even though the cognitive measures were limited in their usefulness as predictors of an arts orientation, the measure of an arts orientation (the Creative Arts scale on the UNIACT) performed quite well in relation to the ratings by experts, both one and three years after the ratings. Although it might not be as stable in upper elementary as in junior high years, an arts orientation does seem to be emerging during this period. It seems to be more closely related to competence (in terms of originality and talent in expression) than to cognitive skill or ability. Originality and technical skill, then, should be assumed to be the leading indicators of an arts orientation, rather than cognitive skills, and early attempts to discover talent should be based on these indicators.

Amabile (1983, pp. 37–63) has perhaps done the most work to establish the reliability of a "consensual assessment technique" to provide an alternative to standardized tests to assess creativity. This technique relies on ratings of artwork by multiple judges, who usually have some degree of expertise. Although Amabile and her colleagues have not always trained judges nor provided them with evaluation criteria, she has been consistently able to arrive at reliability coefficients of .75 to .90 over single tasks (such as rating collages or Haiku poems), indicating a considerable degree of agreement among judges. Agreement may be higher among low or moderate ratings than among high ratings, and it may not be as high over multiple tasks as on a single task (Runco, 1989), but this or a somewhat more structured technique for evaluating creativity needs to be explored as an alternative to objective tests, particularly to assess the artistic creativity of elementary school children.

The second insight gained from this study relates to the nature of problem finding. The creative-thinking exercise (that introduced problem finding) was highly correlated with divergent thinking, but creative thinking was a better predictor of various criteria of creativity and artistic competence than was divergent thinking. It appears that *problem finding requires skills or abilities that were not assessed by the IQ measures, but that at the same time were correlated with achievement and creativity criteria.* Getzels and Jackson (1962, pp. 26–28) noted similar findings with respect to achievement among their group of 26 "high creative" in comparison to "high IQ" adolescents. Getzels and Jackson found that achievement scores of the creative group matched those of the highly intelligent group. Even though they were working with divergent-thinking tests, their explanation still seems valid: The finding "may be related to excellence in cognitive functions not sampled by standard intelligence tests" (p. 27).

What might these other cognitive functions be? What the task in the Kilby study suggests is that the more creative children were superior in intuitive perception than the less creative children. Recall here that intuitive perception is the term MacKinnon (1978, pp. 130–131) used to describe perception that is not stimulus-bound, but stimulus-free and capable of perceiving possibilities rather than just realities. This form of perception is called for on divergent-thinking tasks (e.g., Getzels & Jackson, 1962, pp. 127–128), but when problem finding is involved in the task, intuitive perception seems to be called for to a greater degree. If the reality of the blank card were uniquely to be perceived, the result might be what corresponds to "writer's block:" anxiety that prevents effectively dealing with the situation.

Other cognitive skills or personality characteristics that may contribute to creative thinking (such as imagination and independence) appeared to contribute about equally to creative and divergent thinking. One personality characteristic that appeared to differentiate creative from divergent thinking was the GIFT scale labeled Many Interests. Items on this scale indicated many hobbies, interest in making up stories and in art, and interest in other times and places. The difference in correlations with creative versus divergent thinking was not a result of the item to assess interest in art ("I like to paint pictures"), which all except one student endorsed, but of interests in hobbies and other times and other people. This result suggests that many interests are derived from openness to experience, which is another characteristic of creative individuals (MacKinnon, 1978, p. 129).

The third insight gained related to the nature of the divergent-thinking tests used, and what they measure. They differed from the creative-thinking exercises in their significant correlations with both verbal and nonverbal intelligence measures. Also of interest was their somewhat higher correlation with verbal ability (as measured by the WISC-R Vocabulary scale) than with nonverbal ability (as measured by WISC-R Block Design scale). *The divergent-thinking exercise used in this study seemed to have a verbal bias that was absent from the creative-thinking exercise.* This finding contrasts with the results of Wallach and Kogan for the verbal and performance WISC-R scales in their study, which were neither positively nor differentially correlated with frequency of response to patterns or lines. This contradiction is puzzling, because all of the measures adopted from the Wallach and Kogan study were administered as reported in that study.

These results do confirm the hypothesis that at least in some studies, some divergent-thinking measures calling for verbal response have a verbal bias that renders positive correlation with ratings of drawings for artistic merit less likely. Verbal measures of divergent thinking do not correlate well with measures of visual imagination (McHenry & Shouksmith, 1970). Neither does the verbal bias of some divergent-thinking measures render correlation with arts interest in general more likely, because arts interest does not necessarily share the verbal bias. Arts interest in this study did not correlate significantly or differentially with verbal versus nonverbal intelligence (.09 vs. .13).

The point is important for theory because the hypothesis derived from the definition of creativity focuses on the "openness" of the creative-thinking exercise as an explanation of its validity. If verbal bias, rather than open-endedness, were the principal cause of the correlation of divergent-thinking exercises with creativity criteria, one would not expect that increasing the initial openness of the exercise would have a positive effect on the response as a correlate of creativity. But it did.

The possibility of verbal bias in the criterion (i.e., an arts orientation) was significant enough that a rather careful search of the evidence of the validity of the ACT Creative Arts interest scale was made to determine whether or not correlational differences between verbal and nonverbal achievements could be detected with samples of over 1,000 subjects (Lamb & Prediger, 1981, pp. 40–41). Although a higher percentage of females than males express interest in the arts, this sex bias is minimized on the UNIACT, and would not, if it existed, be *prima facie* evidence of verbal bias, which could more directly be determined in relation to indices of verbal versus nonverbal achievements in the arts.

Little evidence of such bias in correlations of the arts interest scale with achievements was found in the search of validity data. Correlations of scores on the Creative Arts scale with achievements in writing versus art reflected a significant difference for males (.36 vs. .26) but a negligible one for females (.34 vs. .31). When correlations were compared for speech versus music, differences were virtually nonexistant for both males and females. A pattern of differences in the correlations would indicate a verbal bias in the Creative Arts scale, but no significant pattern was found.

The exoneration of this scale from the suspicion of verbal bias is important with respect to its use in other studies described in later chapters. The failure to use an unbiased criterion and the use of a verbally bised creative-thinking task would result in the possibility that all that had been demonstrated through the correlations was a verbal bias in the creative-thinking measure and the criterion, not a relationship between problem-solving skills and arts interest.

As mentioned earlier, this technical point is important, but one can get so bogged down in technicalities that the overall picture becomes obscured. The overall picture in the Kilby study suggests that *in the long run, many determinants other than thinking skills affect developing career orientations.* Artistic competence in the elementary years has already been singled out as the best predictor of an arts orientation as children enter high school. In addition, children's home environment, school environment, and even their community and society may influence their developing career orientation. The six-year follow-up hints at such factors: different home environments, the closing of a small art school, the ethos of a high school, a newspaper contest that displays talent to the community, and so on. The three- and six-year follow-ups reveal that thinking skills may only indirectly influence the development of an arts orientation.

EPILOGUE

Several years after the report of initial findings, Runco and Okuda (1988) found that response to opportunities to discover problems during divergent-thinking tasks accounted for a significant amount of variance in scores on a criterion of creativity when such variance was statistically separated from variance explained by divergent thinking. This finding confirmed that the opportunity to discover or invent a problem does enhance the validity of divergent-thinking tests as measures of creativity.

The findings of this study did not represent a replication as much as an extension of the findings from the Kilby study. Runco and Okuda studied scientifically talented high school students using different measures of divergent thinking (Uses, Instances, and Similarities) and a broader and more behaviorally oriented criterion of creativity (a self-report of accomplishments in science and the creative arts). Despite its differences from the Kilby study, Runco and Okuda's study made the same point with respect to theory: Problem finding and divergent thinking both contribute to creative thinking through the conditions different types of task impose on thought.

Both studies included problem situations that were relatively unconstrained or unformulated, but both also provided contexts in terms of the type of problem to be solved. In addition, both studies required divergent problem solving before asking subjects to invent problems, and limited problem invention tasks to one per type of problem. These technical similarities between studies were not insignificant, and may have been as important to the success of each study as was the subject sample and the choice of a criterion.

chapter 3
Classification of Cognitive Skills

The different types of cognitive skills involved in both finding and solving problems can be specifically described through a classification system. Problems might be classified by their well-defined or ill-defined initial or goal states as in the information-processing approach to problem solving (Meyer, 1983, pp. 5–6; Reitman, 1964, 1965). Alternatively, problems may be classified according to the different situations they pose the problem solver with regard to what is known by whom (Getzels, 1975; Getzels & Csikszentmihalyi, 1967). Because the purpose of the classification here is to refine the definition of creative thinking offered in Chapters 1 and 2, the classification scheme is based on what Reitman called "constraints" on a problem and its solution. This classification was developed independently from the information-processing approach, however, and does not share the limitations of information-processing descriptions of cognitive processes available to find and solve problems.

If constraints on a problem and its solution are each ranged along continua from "closed" to "open," the result is a fourfold classification of problem situations based on the degree of constraint imposed on problems and their solutions. The resulting classes of problems are (a) closed problems with closed solutions, (b) open problems with closed solutions, (c) open problems with open solutions, and (d) closed problems with open solutions. Because continua, not dichotomies, underlie this analysis, discussion of "open" and "closed" situations should be understood to be relational and examples never to be paradigmatic of any class of problem.

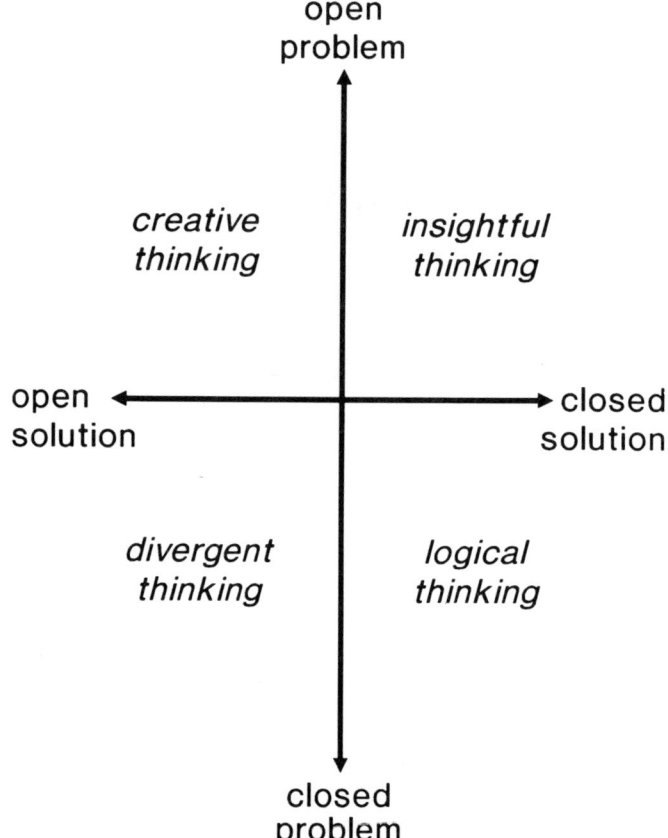

Figure 3.1. Problem finding and solving situations.

CLOSED PROBLEMS WITH CLOSED SOLUTIONS

Problems and solutions that present "closed" as opposed to "open" situations would be classified in the lower cell on the right. In Reitman's (1964) theory, these problems would be well defined: problems that are clearly formulated and that can be solved through a specific, known procedure, with the solution evaluated against an agreed-upon standard. Examples of such problems are common in mathematics and science in school ($7+3=$_____; $8+3x=40-50x$; or conducting a prepared chemistry experiment to obtain desired results). Although such problem solving often calls for domain-specific knowledge, the more general cognitive skills that "closed" or well-defined problems seem to call for are logic or evaluation.

Problems in deductive logic are good examples of well-defined problems because the information given is both necessary and sufficient to arrive at a correct answer. Ennis and Paulus (1965) identified several kinds of reasoning that might be called deductive: sentence logic (in which the basic units are sentences), class logic (in which the basic units are subjects and predicates), ordinal logic (in which the basic units are different degrees or sizes), and several lesser-known types. The criteria for judging arguments in conditional logic (a subtype of sentence logic) and class logic are among the most fully developed and agreed-upon, so these two types of argument are commonly included as a part of convergent or "critical" thinking.

The following is an example of a problem in deductive logic designed to test application of a specific principle of conditional reasoning:

> Given:
> *If the stove is hot, then it is purple.*
> *The stove is not hot.*
> Then, would this conclusion be valid?
> *The stove is not purple.*

The logical principle involved is "given an if-then sentence, the denial of the if-part does not by itself (as the result of its being an if-part) imply the denial of the then-part" (Ennis & Paulus, 1965, Chapt. II, p. 10). The information given is both necessary and sufficient to converge on the correct solution. In the example, the conclusion is invalid, and the answer is "no."

One may contend that such problems test evaluative skills rather than reasoning skills because the person who solves the problem does not produce a deduction. If one concedes this point, the premise that such an item poses a well-defined problem is unaffected. Logico-evaluative constraints on thought are stringent in comparison to those imposed by other types of problems.

The difficulty lies not in validating the construct of a logical-thinking item, but in charting the development of skills to solve it. Many psychologists who have studied this type of thinking have noted that it seems to develop throughout the years of formal education (e.g., Inhelder & Piaget, 1958). An understanding of deductive logic has not fully developed by 11 or 12 years of age, and complete mastery of it may not be achieved by most students even at 17 or 18 (Ennis & Paulus, 1965; Schwabel, 1975).

This developmental progression creates difficulties in the assessment of deduction (noted long ago by Piaget) and requires distinctions between deduction and domain-specific knowledge on the one hand and deduction and several common measures of intelligence on the other. Achievement batteries, for example, do not usually measure deduction, even though solving most problems can be assisted through deductive reasoning (e.g., the systematic elimination of alternatives in multiple-choice questions). On the other hand, IQ is a useful concept for predicting school success, but its equation with deduction is misleading. Scores on IQ subtests of memory capacity (such as those for digit span or serial arrangements of beads) are not as dependent on cognitive development as deduction is. IQ does not generally increase during the school years, whereas deductive reasoning improves, with "remarkable growth" between sixth and eighth grades (Roberge & Paulus, 1971), corresponding to the advanced developments in formal operational thought (Inhelder & Piaget, 1958).

Although the development of deductive thinking can be enhanced by instruction (Ennis & Paulus, 1965), such instruction may not be able to accelerate development a great deal (Nagy & Griffiths, 1982). The most effective mode of instruction is still the subject of much debate (Ennis, 1989; Sternberg & Kastoor, 1986).

OPEN PROBLEMS WITH CLOSED SOLUTIONS

Much less is known about open problems with closed solutions, which can be identified with the situation at the upper right of Figure 3.1. Among his examples, Reitman (1964) noted that of a scientist who wants to account for a phenomenon just observed. Meyer (1983, p. 6) suggested that this type of problem has a poorly defined given state and a well-defined goal state. Mackworth (1965) seemed to have been speaking of such problems when he introduced the concept of problem finding as "close to the heart of originality in creative thinking in science" (p. 54). The given state is essentially empty, while the goal state is reasonably well specified through a formulation that accounts for the facts.

Insight as a term has fallen on hard times in psychology, but it appears that both the original Gestaltists (e.g., Wertheimer, 1982) and more recent revisionists (Davidson & Sternberg, 1984; Sternberg & Davidson, 1983) have used *insight* to describe a thinking skill evoked by this type of problem:

> *A ladder hangs over the side of a ship so that its bottom rung is one inch above the water. Its rungs are eight inches apart. How many rungs will be under water when the tide has risen three feet?*

Such problems may call for selective information processing, but the selection of information relevant to the solution assumes that there is one and only one correct solution. This assumption then engages the problem solver in a search for a more clearly formulated problem, which requires the inference that the ladder on the ship rises with the tide. The formulation of the problem may vary from individual to individual, and may involve imagination or other nonlogical variables in setting the problem (e.g., visualizing the boat and ladder rising with the tide), but the solution is invariant. One knows that the goal state is well defined through a criterion of correctness. The answer to the question is "none."

A number of interesting attempts to identify processes at work in the solution to open problems with closed solutions have recently been undertaken. Smilansky (1984), for example, set high school students the task of inventing matrix items for an IQ test. He found that in this case problem finding differed from but was dependent on the logical ability to solve matrix problems. Smilansky and Halberstadt (1986) also found that problem finding was unrelated to divergent thinking, which is called for when open-ended problems require the generation of multiple alternatives (the fourth type of situation described below). Subotnik (1988) took a related but somewhat more applied approach by studying problem finding among Westinghouse Science Contest winners. She found that convergent thought processes (i.e., deductive logic) were rated as useful for solving the problems these young scientists set for themselves, but divergent thought processes were not rated as useful as the convergent ones.

What these approaches have in common is the type of problem studied, which must be formulated by the problem solver, but which—once formulated—has relatively well-established solution procedures and criteria for evaluating the solution. In other words, the problems, once formulated, call for convergent thinking in the solution process. Although such problems do not seem to call for divergent thinking, they initially seem to call for nonlogical cognitive abilities that are not yet well understood. These may include some of the same abilities useful in creative thinking, but the expressiveness of the solution is constrained by a criterion of correctness.

OPEN PROBLEMS WITH OPEN SOLUTIONS

Problems and solutions which present "open" as opposed to "closed" situations would be identified with the situation at the upper left of Figure 3.1. Reitman (1964) recognized the existence of such "ill-defined" problems, which are difficult to formulate, have few clues for solution procedures, and have less definite criteria for determining a solution than do well-defined problems. Cognitive psychologists have recognized that such situations are often—and perhaps always—involved in real-world tasks that call for creative responses, such as composing a fugue (Reitman, 1964) or composing a painting or a novel (e.g., Glass, Holyoak, & Santa, 1979, pp. 394–397). These situations can also be involved in test response when the respondent has freedom to create the item, and when the solution is open-ended. Such conditions exist when a subject invents and then responds to his or her own divergent-thinking test item, as described in Chapter 2, or when one imagines a picture and tells a story about it, as for the blank card (Card 16) of the *Thematic Apperception Test* (described in Chapter 6).

Truly creative problems have no single criterion for evaluating the correctness of the solution, but seem to be solved expressively. Expression leads one away from the information-processing approach to the analysis of problems and toward the territory of art criticism and emotions. Expression in art is related to the layman's meaning of a "facial look which conveys a feeling" (cf. Chapter 2), but is more technical in meaning. Goodman (1976, p. 95), for example, defines expression as the metaphoric conveyance of properties. The properties mentioned by Goodman and others are often related to emotions or feelings, such as "gaiety, anger, conflict, passion, pride, and pomp and circumstance" (Gardner, 1982, p. 58). The relevant properties are not restricted to emotions, and may include ideas (such as angularity or fluidity). The critical attribute of the metaphor or symbol is its aptness to convey a property, or what psychologists might call its meaningfulness. One criterion for the solution of an artistic problem, then, is not correctness but meaningfulness. Meaningfulness or repleteness is, of course, only one criterion that an expressive solution in art must meet, but it is a necessary criterion.

According to the definition in Chapter 2, the type of thinking called for by open-problem-and-solution conditions is creative thinking, insofar as thinking makes progress under open conditions toward an expressive or meaningful (rather than a correct) solution. When thought does not make such progress, it cannot be called creative. In this manner, individuals who become glib, insincere, digressive, disconnected, or otherwise responsive without regard to meaning can be distinguished from creative thinkers. Such relatively meaningless discourse is frequent enough among us to have inspired at least some educational psychologists to criticize large-scale testing of creative thinking for its failure to control for responses which are not replete with meaning (Ausubel, Novak, & Hanesian, 1978). With only a few exceptions (e.g., Csikszentmihalyi, 1988), creativity researchers have been reluctant to acknowledge the possibility of problematic responses under open-constraint conditions.

CLOSED PROBLEMS WITH OPEN SOLUTIONS

A fourth category of problems are those that are closed, yet have open solutions (the cell at the lower left of Figure 3.1). Reitman (1964) cited the example of an electronics firm that wanted to redesign its product to meet the lower price of a similar product from a competitor. Another example is to redesign a car to obtain better gas mileage. Meyer (1983, p. 5) indicated that this type of problem has a well-defined initial state but a less well-defined goal state. The problem is specified, but the solution is not.

Problems on divergent-thinking tests seem to be of this type, in which interpretations are supplied for patterns or lines presented to the examinee, or uses for some common object (such as a brick) are called for, or multiple consequences are imagined for some unusual event (e.g., "What if ice were to sink rather than float?"). In all of these cases, the problem is presented to rather than invented by the examinee but the solution is open-ended or ill-defined.

There is some evidence from research on divergent thinking that open-ended problems are similar to creative problems with respect to their solution, that is, the solution is expressive in nature. For example, in his studies of convergers versus divergers, Hudson (1966) found that

> One point seems established beyond much dispute. Namely, that there are processes of restriction or inhibition active in the converger, and that these prevent him from expressing (and probably experiencing) a wide range of the feelings to which the diverger is open. (p. 89)

Divergent problem solving appears to be expressive because it reflects the emotional state of the respondent in relation to the task. Direct evidence of the expressive nature of divergent thinking has been obtained from a study with kindergarteners (Singer & Whiton, 1971). Divergent-thinking scores of the children were positively related to the expressiveness of their drawings of people. Less direct evidence of the relation between expression and divergent thinking can be found in the influence of motivation or training on divergent-thinking scores. Harrington (1975) found that college students told to "be creative" responded with scores of markedly increased validity, indicating that anxiety or deficits in self-confidence depressed scores of creative subjects under normal testing conditions. Finally, training that increases divergent-thinking scores has been found to affect mood, increasing group participation, smiles, and humor (Firestein & McCowan, 1988).

The manner in which divergent thinking manifests expression can be summarized as follows. First, expression on a divergent-thinking exercise seems to be restricted to a single dimension of response—less or more. Second, low scores, which may indicate lack of divergent-thinking skill, seem also to reflect expression of sadness, resentment, anxiety, or any sense of weakness in relation to the problem. For this reason, divergent-thinking test authors have frequently stressed gamelike administration conditions (cf. Hattie, 1977; Wallach, 1985). Third, high scores can and perhaps always do reflect highly motivated states, which can stem from positive emotions such as joy, happiness, or confidence, or from any feeling of strength in relation to the task. Fourth, as in creative thinking, the criterion for evaluating the response is meaningfulness. Typically, the meaningfulness of divergent-thinking test response is approached in a nonmetaphoric or a literal manner, as in Line or Pattern Meanings (Wallach & Kogan, 1965) or by screening out bizarre responses during scoring (Torrance, 1974b).

USES OF THE CLASSIFICATION OF COGNITIVE SKILLS

The skill classification system has several purposes. Most importantly, it permits comprehension of a variety of cognitive skills in relation to each other. When these skills are artificially separated in the course of analysis, they seem to offer competing approaches to the study of creativity, when competition is not necessary. The best example is the competition between research on problem finding and divergent thinking. Both problem finding and divergent thinking have been correlated with reasonable criteria of creativity (Barron & Harrington, 1981). On the one hand, problem finding is characteristic of two types of problems in the classification scheme: insight problems (open problems with closed solutions) and creative problems (open problems with open solutions). On the other hand, divergent thinking is a response to a specific problem and solution situation (closed problem, open solution). Divergent thinking does not call for problem finding, but it resembles creative thinking with respect to the expressive nature of the solution.

A second use for the classification scheme is to extend interpretation of research findings. For example, Amabile (1979, 1985) has conducted extensive research on the effects of external evaluation on creative production. In this research, subjects were asked to construct a collage that communicates a feeling of silliness (Amabile, 1979) or to write a Haiku poem (Amabile, 1985). On the surface, these problems would appear to be classified in Reitman's scheme as "ill-defined" because no collage or poem preexisted, and the criteria for evaluating solutions were unknown to most participants.

The classification of a problem and its solution, however, is influenced by perception. In one study, Amabile (1979) found that the expectation of external evaluation among four of five treatment groups diminished the creativity of their collages in comparison with the collages of three control (nonevaluation) groups. The fifth treatment group was given the specific criteria by which creative quality was to be judged *before* they began, and their artwork was judged to be more creative than products made under control conditions.

The classification scheme offers a means to interpret these findings from a problem-solving perspective. In all five treatment groups, perception of the problem situation was affected by the expectation of evaluation, but in different ways. In four of the five groups, the threat of external evaluation seemed to result in constraints on both problem finding and expressive problem solving. Under such constraints, thought appears to have taken "well-worn cognitive pathways" (Amabile, 1979, p. 222) rather than creative directions as in the control groups. In the treatment group that was provided the specific evaluation criteria beforehand, the task seemed to have been perceived as an insight task rather than as a creative task. Evidence that insight rather than creative thinking was evoked by an "evaluation, specific creativity focus" was the evaluation of their collages as vastly superior when compared with collages produced by the control groups.

A third use of the classification scheme is for hypothesis generation. For example, in a series of experiments designed to test the effects of emotional state on problem-solving skills, Jausovec (1989) used Reitman's (1965) and Wakefield's (1989) distinctions between problem types to test the hypothesis that a positive emotional state facilitates the solution of ill-defined problems, but not the solution of well-defined problems. He induced positive and negative affects in different groups of subjects through comic or tragic film segments, then posed to subjects the tasks of solving different types of problems, comparing the results with a control group that had experienced a neutral film segment.

One problem called for the use of analogical reasoning to design a new roof that would decrease energy costs. As Reitman (1964) noted for a similar example, the object had yet to be invented, so the initial state was empty, and the goal state was not clearly defined. Jausovec hypothesized that under such creative conditions, positive affect should facilitate problem solving. Indeed, he found that subjects in a positive emotional state solved the problem significantly more often than subjects in the control group, and tended to solve it more often than subjects in the negative affect treatment group, although this second comparison did not reach statistical significance. A follow-up experiment that required similarly prepared subjects to solve a well-defined problem resulted in no differences between groups. These two experiments illustrated the role of emotions in solving creative-thinking problems of an analogical type, as opposed to solving well-defined problems.

The significance of Jausovec's (1989) experiments for creative thinking in general rests on Guilford's (1967, p. 213) acknowledgment that divergent thinking probably involves transfer. All problem solving that involves expression may involve cognitive mediation of expression through the effects of emotional states on transfer. Emotional states such as happiness are manifested in the abundance of transfer, but emotional states such as apathy or sadness are manifested in the absence of transfer.

The significance of this discovery for the arts appears to be the identification of transfer as one process through which artistic expression is cognitively mediated. For example, happiness is frequently expressed through abundant color or wordage, because these images and behaviors are plausible effects of facilitated transfer. Similarly, sadness is frequently expressed through absent color (black) or parsimonious wordage because these images and behaviors are plausible effects of inhibited transfer. If a feeling is conveyed through metaphor, its conveyance is the result of how we think and act in different affective states, not just how we feel. Put another way, the relationship between the artistic symbol and the property that it expresses is not arbitrary or entirely determined by convention or sense impressions. The aptness or meaningfulness of the metaphor is influenced by how we think.

At this point, much is still not known about deductive logic, insight, creative thinking, or divergent thinking in relation to each other or in relation to other variables of interest. Theoretical elaboration will be deferred in favor of research on the interrelationships of the different cognitive skills, and on their relations to other variables, including the arts orientation.

chapter 4
Creative Thinking at Age Fourteen

> The year I was finishing the eighth grade, I asked our washwoman's daughter what she was going to do when she grew up. She said she didn't know. I said very definitely—as if I had thought it all out and my mind was made up—"I am going to be an artist." (O'Keefe, 1976, n.p.)

The decision by O'Keefe to become an artist in intermediate adolescence seems to be fairly typical of artists, whose vocational interests (along with those of future scientists) tend to crystallize earlier than those of their peers (Tyler, 1964). One is tempted to infer from earlier chapters that such precocious decisions are the result of cognitive skills. Inhelder and Piaget (1958, pp. 341–350) hypothesized a relationship between cognitive development and career planning, but as Vondracek and Lerner (1982) emphasized, almost no empirical work has been done in this area. High school students who are more vocationally mature are also more intelligent (Jordaan & Heyde, 1979, p. 194; Super & Overstreet, 1960, p. 106), and arts students in particular receive more encouragement than average in career planning (Scott, 1988). O'Keefe's comment suggests caution, however, because cognitive skills may not always be involved in the choice of an artistic career, and students from middle-class homes are more likely to be vocationally mature than students from working-class homes (Jordaan & Heyde, 1979, p. 194).

With so little known about the relation between cognitive development and career development, a study of the relationships between cognitive skills and career interests of intermediate adolescents must necessarily involve guesswork as well as hypothesis testing. What measures of logic, divergent thinking, and creative thinking are appropriate for 14-year-old boys and girls? Should one expect the same interrelationships of cognitive skills at 14 as at 11? Would changes in these relationships reflect cognitive development? These were just some of the questions which faced my own investigation of the creative thinking of 14-year-old individuals.

The classification of thinking skills into four categories, described in Chapter 3, led directly to a systematic study of the interrelationships of thinking skills, and the relationships between thinking skills and other variables. Of primary interest were the interrelationships of thinking skills. Because the participants were on average only 14 years old, it was uncertain whether or not relationships between cognitive skills and career interests would be mature.

THE EMPIRICAL INVESTIGATION

The Kilby study, as well as the literature on the emergence of career interests, suggested that vocational interests begin to crystallize in what might be called intermediate adolescence, corresponding with Super's (1963) "tentative" substage of career exploration. The age of 14, which marks this substage, is generally reached in eighth grade, or shortly thereafter.

Relatively complete data sets were obtained from 79 eighth graders with IQs of 85 or above. The preliminary problem was how to select subjects from this group whose responses would be relatively sincere, both to the interest survey and to the "open" conditions on several of the tests. Guidelines provided by the ACT for excluding responses on the basis of insincerity seemed to be devised for older students rather than those 13 years and 9 months, the precise average age of the participants in this study. After considerable doubt about whether or not to use the ACT criteria (which would have excluded the scores of only two participants), a deviation score approach was adopted as the best means to exclude biased data sets.

The deviation score was calculated in the following manner. First, interest scores were converted into stanines for each participant using ACT conversion tables for Grades 8–10. Each participant was then assigned an average interest score, indicating to what extent the participant liked *all* of the activities listed in the survey. Then these average interest scores were normed (norm = 4.97, SD = 1.30), and average interest scores beyond two standard deviations above or below the mean were excluded from further calculations on the basis of an extreme "like" or "dislike" bias, possibly a reflection of insincerity. In other words, average interest scores at or below stanine 2.37 or at or above stanine 7.57

were excluded. A total of 5 participants (2 boys and 3 girls) had such extreme scores, close to the 5 percent of a normal sample found by the ACT to violate their guidelines for an acceptable range of scores. The remaining 74 participants (37 boys and 37 girls) remained the subjects of the study.

Of these 74 subjects, 21 (28%) had "high-point" arts interest. These students were labeled "arts-oriented." Fourteen subjects (18%) were oriented to social services, 16 (21%) were oriented to business contact, 3 (4%) were oriented to business operations, 7 (9%) were oriented to technical careers, and 16 (21%) were oriented to science. The total number of orientations (77) exceeded the number of subjects (74) because the high-point interests of 3 subjects were ties between two areas.

The principal instruments were the unisex edition of the *American College Testing Program Interest Inventory* (UNIACT), the *Stanford Achievement Test*, the *Otis-Lennon School Ability Test*, and four cognitive skills tests designed for the study. The *ACT Interest Inventory* was described in Chapter 1. Raw scores on the UNIACT were converted into stanines for computations. Scale scores on the *Stanford Achievement Test* were obtained for Language, Mathematics, Social Science, and Science. SAIs were obtained from a simultaneous administration of the *Otis-Lennon School Ability Test*. The four cognitive skills tests constructed for the study were a test of deductive logic, a test of insight, a test of creative thinking, and a test of divergent thinking. The compositions of these skills tests are described below. Psychometric properties of the tests from the study are presented with the results.

The test of logical deduction (corresponding with closed-problem and closed-solution situations) was constructed from conditional- and class-reasoning items for Grades 7–12 published by the Instructional Objectives Exchange (1971). This 15-minute test consisted of two practice items and 40 syllogisms (valid or invalid), two items for each of 12 principles of conditional reasoning and two items for each of 8 principles of class reasoning (Ennis & Paulus, 1965, Chapt. II, pp. 10–13). An example of a conditional-reasoning item from this test was provided earlier. The score on the logic test was the total number of syllogisms correctly identified as valid or invalid. The test was administered to a group ($N=28$) of teachers to assess its optimal reliability. Scores for this group averaged 27.07 (SD=4.47), and the coefficent of reliability was acceptably high (alpha=.83).

The test of insight (corresponding with open-problem, closed-solution situations) was constructed from puzzle problems adapted from various sources (e.g., Gardner, 1978; Sternberg, 1986). This 15-minute test consisted of one practice item (with an explanation of the correct answer) and 20 test items in multiple-choice format. An item from this

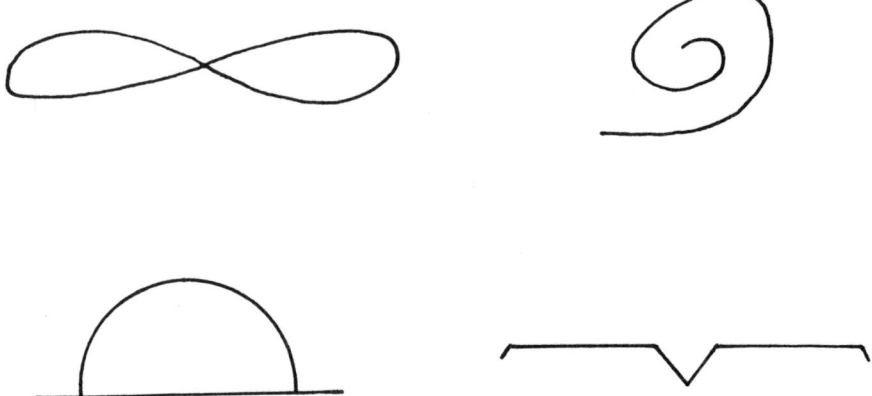

Figure 4.1. Shapes and lines for divergent-thinking exercises.

test was also provided earlier. The score on this test was the total number of correct answers. This test was administered to the same group of teachers on a different occasion ($N = 26$), again to assess optimal reliability. Scores for this group averaged 7.58 (SD = 3.49), and the coefficient of reliability was acceptably high (alpha = .70), although it was somewhat lower than the alpha coefficient for the logic test.

The tests of divergent and creative thinking were structured to permit equal numbers of exercises and time on task. The test of divergent thinking called for divergent associations in response to each of four ambiguous shapes or lines (see Figure 4.1). Subjects had four minutes to write down as many things as they could think of that each shape or line might be, for a total of 16 minutes of divergent-thinking response time. Frequent responses to the shape at the upper left, for example, included "figure eight" and "infinity sign." Less frequent responses included "potato chip" and "holes in a mask." Given that originality and other derived scores on divergent-thinking tests appear to be strongly influenced by quantity of responses (e.g., Clark & Mirels, 1970; Runco & Albert, 1985), only the fluency score (number of responses to all four items) was calculated.

The test of creative thinking called for subjects to design four of their own divergent-thinking items. More specifically, following the presentation of the first two divergent-thinking items (which set the response format), the subjects were asked to do the following:

> Draw a simple shape or form in the space above, then imagine as many things as you can that it could be. Be sure to use the whole drawing in each thing that you write down and not just a part of it. Name only one thing on each line.

Subjects were given four minutes and provided room for 30 responses. In the next exercise, they were asked to follow these instructions:

> Combine the figure that you have just drawn with a different shape or form, then imagine as many new things as you can that your whole drawing could be. Be sure to use all that you have drawn in each thing that you write down and not just a part of it. Name only one thing on each line.

Subjects were again given four minutes. These procedures were repeated after the second two divergent-thinking items were presented, except that subjects were asked to draw lines "of any length or bent" rather than shapes. Subjects were given a total of 16 minutes on the creative-thinking task.

Testing was timed to follow a general assessment of educational progress at the end of the eighth-grade year. Eighth graders in five English classes were informed that participation in a study of vocational interests and thinking skills was voluntary, but that as a benefit of participation they would receive indications of their vocational preferences and examples of corresponding careers.

Students choosing to participate were tested in their English classes over three days. On the first day, they were oriented to the study and given the interest inventory. On the second day, they were given the divergent-thinking and the creative-thinking tests. The third day, they were given the insight and logic tests, and after testing was completed, they were given their Holland (1985a) codes signifying their top three interest areas, examples of appropriate careers, and a reference for further information.

Data analysis was conducted in three steps. First, psychometric characteristics of the cognitive skills tests were calculated for this sample. Second, all variables in the study were intercorrelated. A multiple correlation was calculated with arts interest as the criterion and logic, divergent thinking, and creative thinking as predictor variables. Third, artistically oriented students were separated from the sample and differences between scores for this subgroup and the other subjects were calculated for all variables.

Table 4.1 presents the means and standard deviations of the 15 measures used in the study. Of particular interest are the means and standard deviations of the cognitive skills tests. Random response would have predicted scores of 20 on the logic test (40 items with two alternatives) and 5 on the insight test (20 items with four alternatives). The mean scores on these tests were not far from a random score, indicating that many students were guessing, particularly on the insight test. The ranges of scores on these tests, however, were from 18 to 34 on the logic test and from 2 to 13 on the insight test, indicating that though quite

Table 4.1. Eighth-Grade Means and Standard Deviations

Variable	Mean	SD
School Ability Index (IQ)	112.0	14.8
Stanford Achievement Test (scaled scores)		
Language (Lang)	710.6	32.6
Math	717.1	37.9
Social Science (SoSc)	703.8	39.9
Science (Sci)	689.1	27.1
Cognitive Skills Tests		
Logic (Log)	24.4	3.4
Insight (Ins)	5.7	2.2
Divergent Thinking (DT)	32.4	12.7
Creative Thinking (CT)	31.1	15.5
ACT Interest Scales (norm sample stanines)		
Science (SCI)	5.3	2.1
Creative Arts (CAI)	5.4	2.0
Social Service (SSI)	5.2	1.9
Business Contact (BCI)	5.0	1.8
Business Operations (BOI)	4.4	1.7
Technical (TI)	4.9	1.1

Note: $N = 74$, except for SAI ($N = 69$).

variable around the means, the responses at the extremes discriminated ability.

Reliabilities of the cognitive skills tests were assessed through alpha coefficients calculated from split halves (odd/even). The reliability of the logic test was found to be .58, which was low but was acceptable for exploratory research purposes. The reliability of the insight test was found to be .36, which was too low for much score interpretation. Extreme nonrandom scores on the insight test, however, permitted it to be useful for correlations, so this score was included in further calculations. The reliability of the divergent-thinking test was found to be .89, which was quite high given the limited response time. Finally, the reliability of the creative-thinking test was determined to be .82.

Correlations between cognitive skills are presented in Figure 4.2. Correlations between logic and insight, and between divergent and creative thinking were higher than anticipated, but the configuration of correlations was otherwise not far from what one might expect from the classification scheme. Cross-correlations were low, but correlations between responses to similar types of problem or solution situations were generally higher. The representation of these correlations in Figure 4.2 as an inverse function of distance (the higher the correlation, the shorter the distance) seemed generally apt.

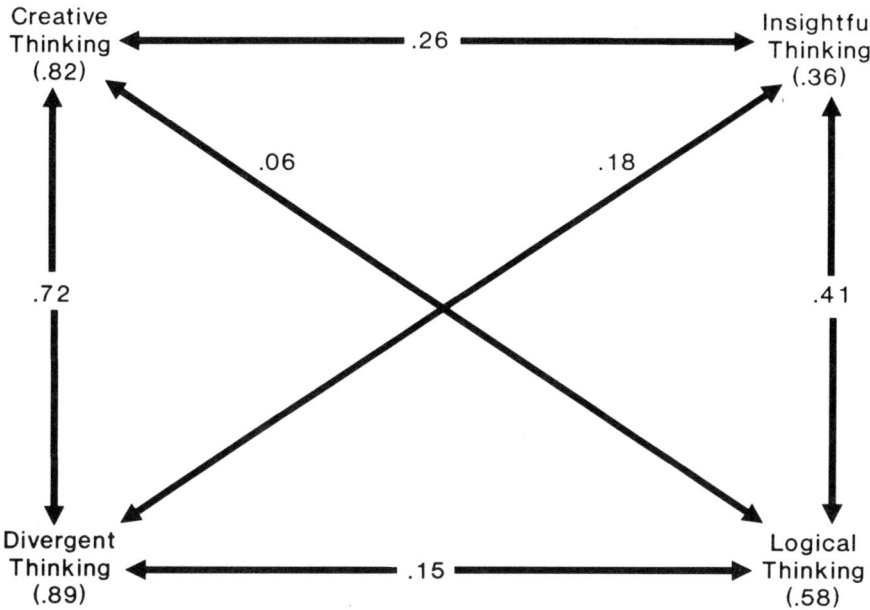

Figure 4.2. Configuration of cognitive skills.

Intercorrelations of cognitive skills as well as most other study variables are reported in Table 4.2. The table lists the tests in an arrangement which parallels Table 2.2 to facilitate comparisons. Four groups of significant correlations should be noted in addition to the intercorrelations of cognitive skills. First, the large number of correlations underscored at the left side of the table indicate intercorrelations between tests that called for convergent thought processes. The similar correlations between the logic test and IQ or achievement measures were indications of the role that convergent thinking played in IQ and achievement test performance. Interestingly, scores on the insight test seemed to be more highly related to general intelligence, mathematics achievement, and logic than to achievements in language, social science, and science, signaling that insight as measured was probably a derivative concept of mathematics.

In a second pattern, scores on convergent-type tests (logic, IQ, and achievement) were found to be related to science career interests. Although the highest correlation in this grouping was between science achievement and science interest, what is striking is the consistency of the correlations. All seemed to be moderately significant.

Third, IQ and math achievement seemed to be significantly, but not strongly correlated with business operations career interests. These correlations seemed to reflect a relationship between skill at solving well-

Table 4.2. Intercorrelation of Variables for Eighth Graders

	Achievements				Cognitive Skills				Interests				
	IQ	Lang	Math	SoSc	Sci	Log	Ins	DT	CT	SCI	CAI	SSI	BCI	BOI	TI
IQ	—	.72	.84	.74	.72	.57	.48	.18	.06	.28	.18	.11	.14	.26	.19
Lang		—	.73	.73	.66	.51	.29	.18	.07	.32	.17	.18	.11	.19	.09
Math			—	.73	.77	.51	.49	.21	.14	.31	.14	.08	.06	.28	.12
SoSc				—	.75	.51	.29	.18	-.04	.31	.12	.07	.14	.22	.19
Sci					—	.51	.24	.11	-.01	.41	.04	-.13	-.08	.19	.18
Log						—	.41	.15	.06	.35	.22	-.07	-.06	-.05	.12
Ins							—	.18	.26	.21	.22	-.10	.00	.03	.07
DT								—	.72	.10	.41	.16	.10	.00	-.02
CT									—	.06	.34	.21	.12	.00	-.14

Notes: Refer to Table 4.1 for complete measure titles. Underscored correlations are significant. With $N=74$, .23 is significant at the .05 level, .30 is significant at the .01 level, and .38 is significant at the .001 level.

Table 4.3. Eighth-Grade Comparisons of Arts-Oriented Students with Other Students

Variable	Arts X	Other X	t
School Ability Index	116.9	110.1	1.77
Stanford Achievement Test			
Language	724.1	705.3	2.32*
Mathematics	733.9	710.5	2.47*
Social Science[a]	718.0	698.2	1.65
Science	698.7	685.2	1.96*
Cognitive Skills Tests			
Logic	25.0	24.1	1.11
Insight[a]	6.0	5.4	.94
Divergent Thinking	37.2	30.5	2.10*
Creative Thinking	35.3	29.5	1.47
ACT Interest Scales			
Science	5.5	5.3	.39
Creative Arts[a]	7.3	4.7	7.72*
Social Service	4.8	5.4	-1.19
Business Contact	5.0	5.0	-0.01
Business Operations	4.4	4.3	.20
Technical	4.9	3.7	2.34*

Note: Arts-Oriented $N=21$, Other $N=53$, except for SAI (20, 49).
[a] t calculated when variances assumed unequal.
*$p<.05$.

defined problems and interest in business operations, which at the same time was not associated with logic. Logic was not correlated with interest in this area.

Fourth, divergent-thinking and creative-thinking scores correlated moderately significantly with arts interest. These correlations were almost the inverse of the correlations reported in Chapter 2. That is, divergent thinking appeared to be somewhat more strongly related to arts interest than was creative thinking.

A multiple correlation was calculated for the model suggested by the literature reviewed in Chapter 1. Arts interest was the criterion variable and logic, divergent thinking, and creative thinking (which incorporated problem finding) were the predictor variables. The resulting coefficient proved to be highly significant ($R=.45$, $F(3,70)=5.78$, $p<.005$). A model with only logic and divergent thinking as predictors, however, was almost as highly predictive of the criterion ($R=.44$) as the model with creative thinking included among three predictors.

As a third step in data analysis, the scores of the 21 subjects with an arts orientation were statistically compared with scores of the other 53 subjects for significant differences on all variables. Table 4.3 presents the results. The arts-oriented subjects differed positively and significantly from the other subjects in respect to divergent thinking, language, math, and science achievements, and arts and technical interests.

IMPLICATIONS

Several implications can be drawn from this attempt to measure the interrelationships between thinking skills and the relationships between thinking skills, achievements, and career interests. First, the measures of thinking skills designed for the study were adequately reliable, with the exception of the insight test. Insight, however, appears from other research (e.g., Arlin, 1975; Smilansky, 1984) to have a developmental relationship to logic: Deductive logic must be mastered before problem finding can emerge in a metacognitive relationship to this skill. The problem, then, appears to have been not so much the measure of insight as the immaturity of insight in relation to logic. The success of the same insight test with teachers was added evidence that insight develops with age and is not a function of intelligence apart from maturity.

Second, the correlations of cognitive skills with achievements and career interests projected patterns for two different types of student. They clearly resembled Hudson's (1966) diverger and converger, although their differences were based on correlations of scores for many individuals, not on the determination of individual cognitive biases. Only two cognitive profiles were found, but others may exist based on different cognitive skills in relation to career interests or based on testing older or more specialized groups of subjects. Some evidence was obtained, in fact, for a third cognitive profile related to business operations.

One of the two clearly delineated types can be labeled the scientifically inclined student. At age 14, this type is better at logical thinking than his or her peers. The logical skill (and perhaps IQ) of the scientifically inclined type is reflected in school achievements in science, language, math, and social science—that is, in virtually all required academic subjects. The scientific student is an academic achiever. On the other hand, the artistically inclined student at age 14 is distinctly better than peers at divergent thinking. The multiple correlations suggest that logic also contributes to the thinking skills of this type of student.

When arts-oriented students were compared with other students, the artistically inclined student also emerged as an academic achiever. Arts-oriented students performed significantly better on most of the achievement tests in comparison to other students. This finding matches the correlational findings for fifth-grade children reported in Chapter 2. The significant school achievements of arts-oriented students are of least in part due to cognitive processes that are not measured by traditional tests of school ability.

The creative-thinking test in the present study was not nearly as well correlated with intelligence as was the creative-thinking measure in fifth grade (.06 vs. .23 and .20). In fact, the creative-thinking test in the present study seemed somewhat artificially to separate nonlogical cognitive processes from deductive logic, which continues to be emergent in the eighth grade. The effect may well have been to depress correlations of creative-thinking scores (as compared to divergent-thinking scores) not only with IQ, logic, and achievement, but also with arts interest, which seemed to be correlated positively but not significantly with deductive logic (.22).

This "flaw" in the creative-thinking measure was actually a feature of the classification of cognitive skills, which distinguished creative from logical thinking. This distinction, although useful for theoretical purposes, may not be realistic, particularly in light of intellectual developments in junior high school. Creative thinking may begin to require a logical element, which in the present study, was better reflected in correlations with divergent-thinking scores rather than with creative-thinking scores. Beginning somewhere in the early teens, artistic problem solving may require logic, even if nonlogical elements (such as intuitive perception) are also required.

Accordingly, work with invented problems among teenagers seems to recommend the invention of a logically related, open-ended problem rather than the invention of associative problems. The invention of associative problems (e.g., drawing one's own pattern or line) may, however, still have its place in a test of theoretical constructs which requires the separation of nonlogical from logical elements of creative test response.

CONCLUSION

The study described in this chapter contributed to our understanding of the relationships of problem-solving skills to the arts orientation by confirming that a pattern of problem-solving skills or abilities is associated with arts interest. Among 14-year-olds, this pattern seems to be emergent rather than established. Nonlogical cognitive skills or abilities are clearly associated with arts interest, but the separation of these skills or abilities from logic appears to weaken the relationship of creative thinking to arts interest.

The theory that was tested proved to have value for identifying tasks that separated cognitive skills or abilities, but several of these skills may in reality operate in concert, particularly in the artistically oriented individual. What the correlations reveal is that in themselves, these skills or abilities are not always closely related.

The study described in this chapter also was able to verify that arts-oriented students think more divergently and achieve more highly in most school subjects than do other students. Higher achievement, as pointed out in Chapter 2, does not necessarily imply higher IQ. The average IQ for arts-oriented students was not far from the total group mean, and it failed to achieve the criterion of significance for a measurable difference from the average IQ of other students.

The implications of the findings for further empirical work include revision of the theory to permit distinct cognitive skills to exist in closer relationship. They also suggest that an investigation is needed with older subjects, who are more intellectually mature. We turn, then, to look at problem-solving skills and the arts orientation at the end of high school.

chapter 5
Creative Thinking of High School Seniors

The literature on vocational development stresses changes in interest between 14 and 18 years, including the appearance of new career interests and the narrowing of career interests. Super (1969) reported in the 12th-grade follow-up to the study of vocational maturity among 9th-grade boys, that as many as 56 percent of the 12th graders had preferences in a field of work quite different from the occupation preferred in 9th grade. Osipow (1973, p. 150) noted, however, that when larger categories of work have been used in other assessments (e.g., Astin, 1967), less change appeared to have occurred over the high school years. Osipow concluded that preferences for one or more large categories over others "may represent a major portion of the type of output measured by standard interest inventories," permitting "planners to develop general curricula oriented around large categories of occupational events" (p. 150).

A second source of variance in interests during the high school years is a narrowing of interest as a result of crystallation of career choice (Jordaan & Heyde, 1979, pp. 185–186). This source is mitigated for arts interest by what appear to be relatively early career decisions, as mentioned at the beginning of Chapter 4. Early crystallation of plans appears to result in greater stability for arts (and science) interest scales when compared with other interest scales during high school and college. In one large high-school study (Cooley, 1967), test-retest reliabilities (combined male and female) for physical- and biological-science interest scales over four years averaged .56. The retest values for arts interest scales (Literary, Artistic, and Musical) had about the same average (.55), but the values for 12 other nonscience interest scales averaged only .49. Similarly differential values are reported by Hansen and Stocco (1980), Lamb and Prediger (1981, p. 26), Holland (1985b, p. 44), and Wakefield (1989).

Even though the effects of changes in and narrowing of interests in high school seem to be mitigated by relatively early career decisions by arts-oriented students, the question still arises: Do these changes of interest in high school affect the relationship of cognitive skills to the arts orientation? To answer this question, some evidence of the relationships of cognitive skills to arts interest was gathered in a study of cognitive skills in relation to career interests in the 12th grade, and a comparison was made between arts-oriented and other seniors in terms of cognitive skills and creative behaviors.

This study differed from the previous one in several respects. Although the classification of cognitive skills introduced in Chapter 3 continued to offer a theoretical framework for analysis of cognitive skills, an attempt was undertaken to improve measures based on earlier results. More specifically, insight, creative-thinking, and divergent-thinking tests were changed in ways specified below.

Earlier research guided the development of specific hypotheses. These hypotheses were not necessarily derived from the classification of cognitive skills, but were consistent with expectations developed from studies of sixth and eighth graders. Finally, an attempt was made to measure creative achievements in different domains. Achievements toward the end of high school in literature, art, the performing arts, crafts, and mathematics or science were measured by a self-report. These differences from the study of eighth graders, it was thought, would improve the interpretability of the results at minimal cost.

The cost was that scores for 12th graders on three of the four cognitive skills tests could not be directly compared with scores on the same tests for eighth graders. Although different groups of students were involved in the two studies, comparison of scores on the same tests might have yielded potentially valuable developmental information. The sacrifice of this potential was justified by potential improvements in the psychometric characteristics of the cognitive skills tests. In addition, developmental comparisons could still be made using the logic test, which was unchanged.

Three hypotheses were generated with specific reference to the arts orientation in the 12th grade:

1. Arts interest should be positively correlated with creative behaviors. This hypothesis was designed to test the concurrent validity of the arts interest scale as a measure of creativity.
2. Arts interest should be positively correlated with logical-, divergent-, and creative-thinking skills. This central hypothesis was derived

from the classsification of cognitive skills (Chapter 3) and from earlier research.
3. Logical-, divergent-, and creative-thinking skills should be positively correlated with creative behaviors. This hypothesis was developed to triangulate the relationships between arts interest and cognitive skills through an alternative measure of creativity.

In addition to these hypotheses, several related expectations were developed for artistically oriented students in comparison to other students. These expectations, however, are discussed after the results are presented for testing the three hypotheses.

THE EMPIRICAL INVESTIGATION

Complete data sets were obtained for 69 twelfth graders two weeks before graduation. Because four interest surveys were invalidated, only 65 of these sets (28 male and 37 female) were included in the study. The ages of the subjects averaged 17 years 8 months. Concurrent IQ and achievement test scores were not available because 12th graders in this system take competency tests rather than an achievement battery.

Ability levels of subjects were estimated from the levels of the English classes in which they were tested. Twenty subjects were in Advanced Placement (AP) English, 29 were in College Bound English, and 16 were in General English. Of the 20 AP English students, all had participated in other AP classes, and half had taken AP calculus. Seven had won awards as seniors in district, regional, or statewide poetry, short story, or essay competitions. At the other extreme, one subject in the College Bound group and four in the General group had failed a grade during their education.

Twelve (18%) of the subjects had high-point interest scores in the creative arts, and as in the study of eighth graders, these subjects were labeled "arts-oriented." Sixteen (24%) of the subjects were oriented to social service, 15 (22%) were oriented to business contact, 7 (10%) were oriented to business operations, 5 (7%) were oriented to technical careers, and 13 (19%) were oriented to science. Once again career orientations (68) outnumbered subjects (65) because 3 subjects each had two interest areas tied for the high-point score.

Permission was again obtained from the American College Testing Program to use the UNIACT. As mentioned in Chapter 4, the criteria supplied by the ACT for designating unclear interests exclude 5 percent of a normal sample, and these criteria were applied, resulting in the data sets of 4 participants being excluded from the study. Raw scores of the

65 remaining interest surveys were converted into stanines using a conversion table for 11th Grade to Adult supplied by the ACT.

Three of the four cognitive skills tests used in the previous study were substantially redesigned. The logic test was the same, but when scores for 12th graders (26.48, SD = 4.65) were statistically compared with scores for 8th graders (24.35, SD = 3.40), the scores of the former were found to be significantly higher ($t = 3.11$, $p < .01$). The reliability of the logic test (alpha = .76) was also somewhat higher for 12th as opposed to 8th grade.

Three items on the insight test were changed to make them easier, and all of the insight items were modified to add a fourth distractor, reducing the random score on this 20-item test to 4. Perhaps partly as a result of these revisions, the insight scores were somewhat higher (6.46, SD = 3.27) and a great deal more reliable (alpha = .71) in 12th than in 8th grade.

The divergent-thinking test was constructed from three items calling for lists of uses, not unlike a divergent-thinking exercise called Unusual Uses (Guilford, Wilson, Christensen, & Lewis, 1951; Wallach & Kogan, 1965; Torrance, 1974a). These exercises were verbal rather than visual, and they bore a relation to convergent thinking through the generation of logically related responses. As divergent-thinking exercises, however, these items differed from convergent-thinking items through the absence of other constraints on the answer (Guilford, 1975).

The divergent-thinking test was administered with these instructions:

> On each of the next three pages, you will have the chance to think up as many uses as you can for some common object, such as a blanket. List as many uses as possible, one on each line. For example, a blanket is normally used to keep a person warm, but it can also be used as a saddle pad, an exercise mat, a playhouse, etc. You will have four (4) minutes to think up as many uses as you can for each object.

Items called for uses other than the usual ones for (a) a quarter, (b) a popsicle stick, and (c) a paper cup. Items were scored for fluency (the number of responses). Scores averaged 18.77 (SD = 7.13) and were quite reliable (alpha = .84).

A creative-thinking test (adapted from Runco & Okuda, 1988) was constructed from three items calling for lists of uses for objects named by the examinee. This test was administered with these instructions:

> On each of the next three pages, you will have a chance to imagine some common objects for which there are many uses. Write the name of the object and its most common use in the space provided, then list as many other uses as you can for that object. The quality of your item will be judged by the number of uses you can think of for the object which you have chosen.

The items called for uses for (a) metal, (b) wooden, and (c) paper objects named by the examinee. Subjects were told in the directions for each item that they had four minutes to respond. This test was also scored for fluency or number of responses. Scores averaged 21.66 (SD = 8.35) and were adequately reliable (alpha = .65).

The instrument to assess creative behaviors was a modified version of the *Creative Behavior Inventory* (Hocevar, 1979, 1980). The CBI is a 90-item survey of activities and achievements in Literature, Music, Performing Arts, Art, Crafts, and Math-Science. The instrument was modified to omit 15 unscalable items, to address achievements in Grades 7–12, and to limit responses to three categories (*never, once or twice, three or more times*). Score averages are reported by Wakefield (1989), and alpha coefficients of the six scales varied from a low of .54 (Math-Science) to a high of .80 (Literature), with the other alpha coefficients falling in the .70s.

High school seniors in five English classes were informed in mid-May that participation in a study of vocational interests and thinking skills was voluntary, but as a benefit of participation they would receive indications of their vocational preferences (Holland codes) and examples of corresponding careers. Students choosing to participate were tested in their English classes over two days. On the first day, they took the UNIACT and were given divergent-thinking and creative-thinking tests. To control for contamination of open-ended items by self-reports, creative-thinking items were relabeled *Item Invention*, and no mention of creativity was made until the second day. At this point, subjects filled out the modified CBI and were given the insight and logic tests. At the end of the second day, all participants were provided with their Holland codes and examples of corresponding careers.

Data were handled using statistical procedures which included several forms of correlation, including multiple correlation (R) and canonical correlation (Rc). A multiple correlation identifies the degree of association between a set of predictor variables and a single-variable criterion, and a canonical correlation identifies the degree of association between a set of predictor variables and a set of criterion variables. Although multiple and canonical correlations are statistical procedures that require the use of a computer, they are more parsimonious than product-moment correlations to describe the combined association of more than two variables (Cohen & Cohen, 1975). These techniques allow a researcher to summarize patterns of association. These patterns can also be identified in tables of product-moment correlations, supplied below.

Figure 5.1 portrays the intercorrelations of the cognitive skills tests in the form of a matrix that reflects the skills classification scheme. In general, the matrix differs from the one portrayed in Chapter 4 in several ways. The reliabilities of the four tests are more homogeneous than in the earlier study, allowing for more interpretation of relationships be-

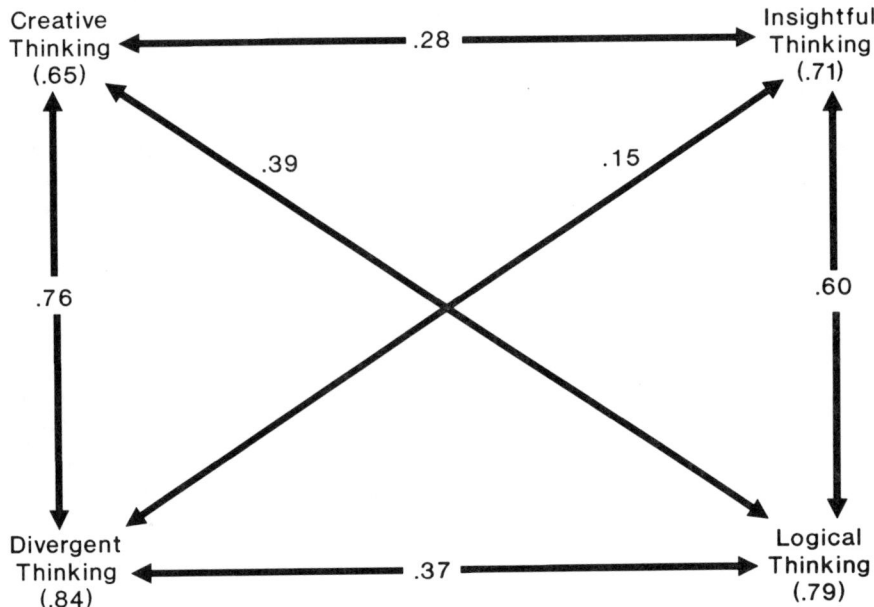

Figure 5.1. Configuration of cognitive skills (revised).

tween skills. All of the correlations are higher (perhaps due in part to higher reliabilities), signaling related (rather than discrete) cognitive skills. Logic and insight were especially closely related, as were divergent and creative thinking.

Two correlations in this figure deserve special attention. One is the correlation between logical and creative thinking. This value is much higher than in the earlier study. This correlation suggests some relationship between these two skills which was absent in the earlier study. The other interesting correlation is between insight and creative thinking. The correlation between these two types of thinking was significant (but difficult to interpret) in the earlier study. Here, however, the effect of logic could be partialed out of the relationship to discover whether or not the residual coefficient was significant. It was not ($r' = .07$), suggesting that the correlation of insight with creative thinking reflected the relationship of both thinking skills to logic, rather than an independently significant association.

Partialing out the effects of intentionally related tests can obscure rather than clarify findings, however, so this procedure was generally not used, with one further exception noted below. Rather, the three hypotheses of the study were approached through tabulations of product-moment correlations and through other statistical procedures. Table 5.1 reports the results of correlating the six UNIACT scales with the six

Table 5.1. Correlations Between Career Interests and Creative Behaviors ($N=65$)

Creative Behaviors	Career Interests					
	Science	Arts	Service	Business Contact	Business Operations	Technical
Literature	.07	.36**	.04	−.10	−.25*	−.06
Music	.19	.39**	.01	−.07	−.11	−.05
Performing Arts	.29*	.35**	.38**	.01	−.23	.05
Art	.13	.38**	−.01	−.20	−.29*	.19
Crafts	.26*	.34**	.23	.10	−.08	.26*
Math-Science	.24	.26*	−.22	.05	.06	.19

* $p < .05$
** $p < .01$

Table 5.2. Correlations Between Career Interests and Cognitive Skills ($N=65$)

Cognitive Skills	Career Interests					
	Science	Arts	Service	Business Contact	Business Operations	Technical
Logical	.15	.37**	.11	.03	−.05	.11
Insightful	.08	.20	−.27*	−.14	−.02	.11
Creative	.21	.35**	.10	.16	−.04	.31*
Divergent	.13	.31*	.18	.19	.02	.38**

* $p < .05$
** $p < .01$

scales of the CBI. Interest in the arts was the only UNIACT scale which correlated positively and significantly with every domain of creative achievement, including Math-Science. Science interest correlated significantly with two domains of creative behavior (Crafts and Performing Arts), but neither value was highly significant. Interest in business operations correlated negatively with achievements in two creative domains (Literature and Art), confirming the construct validity of arts interest, which was theoretically oppositional to business operations interest.

A multiple correlation coefficient was calculated with arts interest as the dependent variable and five creative behavior scales (Literature, Music, Performing Arts, Art, and Crafts) as independent variables. The resulting coefficient was highly significant ($R = .55$, $F(5,59) = 5.19$, $p < .0005$). This multiple correlation provided evidence of the validity of arts interest as a measure of creativity.

Table 5.2 reports the results of correlating the four cognitive skills measures with the six UNIACT scales. Two clusters of significant correlations were obtained, one related to arts interest and the other to technical interest. Logical, creative, and divergent thinking were all found to

Table 5.3. Correlations Between Cognitive Skills and Creative Behaviors (N = 65)

Cognitive Skills	Creative Behaviors					
	Literature	Music	Perf. Arts	Art	Crafts	Math-Science
Logical	.25*	.17	.13	.26*	.08	.31*
Insightful	−.01	.23	−.01	.18	−.18	.34**
Creative	.36**	.14	.14	.40***	.22	.34**
Divergent	.44***	.13	.16	.47***	.37**	.43***

* $p < .05$
** $p < .01$
*** $p < .001$

be significantly associated with arts interest. Partial correlations were calculated to provide an indication of the unique relationships of logical and creative thinking with arts interest. When the effect of creative thinking was partialed out of the relationship between logic and arts interest, a significant value (.27, $p < .05$) remained. When the effect of logic was partialed out of the relationship between creative thinking and arts interest, the residual value (.24) did not meet the criterion for statistical significance. Logic, somewhat more than creative thinking, was found to exist independently in relation to arts interest.

A multiple correlation coefficient was calculated with arts interest as the dependent variable and logical, creative, divergent thinking as independent variables. The resulting coefficient was highly significant ($R = .44$, $F(3,61) = 4.82$, $p < .005$). This correlation provided evidence in support of the central hypothesis, which predicted associations between cognitive skills and arts interest. To provide a more general indication of the association between cognitive skills and career interests, a canonical correlation was calculated with all four cognitive skills as predictor variables and all six career interests as criterion variables. The resulting value ($Rc = .51$, $F(24,193) = 1.60$, $p < .05$) was significant.

Table 5.3 presents the results of correlating the four cognitive skills tests and the six scales of the CBI. Three patterns of correlations were found. First, as expected, cognitive skills correlated significantly with literary and artistic achievements. Second, all cognitive skills correlated significantly with achievements in math or science. Third, no cognitive skill correlated significantly with achievements in three domains of behavior (Music, Crafts, and Performing Arts), with the exception of divergent thinking, which was significantly correlated with achievements in crafts.

A canonical correlation was calculated to estimate the maximum correlation of three predictor variables (logical, divergent, and creative thinking) with a specific set of five criterion variables (Literature, Music, Performing Arts, Art, and Crafts). The resulting coefficeint was signifi-

Table 5.4. Twelfth-Grade Comparisons of Arts-Oriented Students with Other Students

Variable	Arts X	Other X	t
Cognitive Skills Tests			
Logic	28.4	26.0	1.62
Insight	8.3	6.0	2.29*
Divergent Thinking	21.4	18.2	1.44
Creative Thinking	25.2	20.8	1.64
Creative Behavior Inventory			
Literature	7.8	6.2	1.18
Music[a]	6.3	2.7	2.76**
Performing Arts	5.6	2.2	3.28**
Art	5.3	3.5	2.04*
Crafts	15.8	12.8	1.52
Math-Science	3.8	2.5	1.78
ACT Interest Scales			
Science	6.4	5.4	1.44
Creative Arts	7.7	5.1	4.90**
Social Service	5.9	5.8	0.26
Business Contact	5.2	6.1	−1.49
Business Operations	3.3	5.3	−2.82**
Technical	4.3	4.4	−0.20

Note: Arts-Oriented $N=12$, Other $N=53$
[a] t calculated when variances assumed unequal
* $p<.05$
** $p<.01$

cant ($Rc=.56$, $F(15,158)=1.85$, $p<.05$). The coefficeint essentially summarized two of the patterns of correlation cofficients manifested in Table 5.3 and provided some support for the third hypothesis. Cognitive skills, however, appeared to be more strongly associated with literary and artistic achievements than with achievements in music and the performing arts.

Finally, the means on all measures for the 12 arts-oriented subjects were compared with means for the 53 other subjects. The results are portrayed in Table 5.4. Although the number of arts-oriented students was very small (even in comparison to arts-oriented students in the eighth-grade sample), statistically significant differences did appear on some measures. The arts-oriented students scored significantly higher than other students on measures of insight, creative achievement in music, art and performing arts, and arts interest. Arts-oriented students expressed significantly less interest in business operations careers than did the other students. It should be noted that although the test statistic did not reach the criterion for significance, trends toward significant differences were also obtained for logic and creative thinking, and creative achievements in math or science.

IMPLICATIONS

Any detailed discussion of the results of hypothesis testing needs to begin with analysis of the tasks. In this study, cognitive skills tests possessed similar reliabilities, so the results are more interpretable than before. The cognitive skills tests were also more closely interrelated than those used in previous investigations, making the presence and absence of correlations with other measures more poignant and revealing. The revisions of the tests permit some new conclusions to be reached, but at the cost of preventing conclusions about the development of most of the thinking skills involved.

The one variable that did reveal what appears to have been developmental progress is deductive logic. The 12th-grade sample scored significantly higher on this variable than did the 8th-grade sample. Although matched intellectual ability would have been necessary if the study had set out to demonstrate this development, other studies (e.g., Roberge & Paulus, 1971) that have set out to measure age-related changes have found significant development of conditional and class reasoning beyond the 8th grade. The continued development of logic justified the changes in the creative- and the divergent-thinking measures from the associative measures used with the 8th graders.

More so than in previous studies, then, creative thinking appeared to be dependent on logical thinking. Inventing a logically based divergent-thinking item required logic to a surprising degree. The relative unreliability of response to the creative-thinking task may have indicated that problem finding in a logical mode is not fully mature at the end of high school. Alternatively, this relative unreliability may be a function of the openness of the item construction conditions. Throughout earlier studies, responses to item-invention tasks have been consistently less reliable than responses to more conventional items, even when time on task has been equated. Whether the relative unreliability of the creative-thinking measure in the present study resulted from immature logical problem-finding ability or the increased openness of the creative-thinking as opposed to the divergent-thinking task cannot be determined without further research on problem invention. So little is known about such tasks that they represent an entirely new area of research.

The first formal hypothesis of the study—that arts interest would be associated with creative behaviors—was supported both in unique correlations of arts interest with creative behaviors and in a substantial multiple correlation of arts interest with creative behaviors. The positive and significant correlations in Table 5.1 are very similar to those between the UNIACT Creative Arts scale and out-of-class accomplishments in music, art, and writing by college bound high school students (Lamb & Prediger, 1981, p. 40). In general, the correlations in Table 5.1 differ from those in the UNIACT norms report only in respect to the negative correlations found between business operations interest and creative behaviors in literature and art, which in the ACT report were not significant (.00 and −.06 for writing; −.06 and −.07 for art).

The multiple correlation (.55) calculated for the present study, then, is a fairly good indication of what the cumulative effect would have been of the separate correlations between arts interest and out-of-class accomplishments in areas such as music, speech, art, and writing in the UNIACT norms report. In fact, the multiple correlation obtained in this study is very similar to intercorrelations obtained between the two subscales of Holland's *Self-Directed Search* which most nearly resemble the activities listed in UNIACT and the extracurricular accomplishments listed in the CBI. These subscales (Artistic Activity and Artistic Competency) are highly intercorrelated for both men and women (.44 and .63; Holland, 1985b, p. 40).

The second hypothesis, which was central to the study, anticipated that three distinguishable cognitive skills would be correlated with arts interest, that is, the measure of the arts orientation used in this and previous studies. This hypothesis was largely confirmed through both bivariate and multiple correlations. Logic correlated somewhat more highly with arts interest than anticipated, and the differential between the correlations of creative and divergent thinking with arts interest was not as great as anticipated, but the hypothesis found overall support in both the level of statistical significance reached by all three correlations and by the absence of correlations of cognitive skills with other types of interest. The positive correlations of divergent and creative thinking with technical interest appear to have been a method effect of the "uses" exercises, and might be expected to disappear if a wider range of divergent-thinking and creative-thinking exercises were employed.

The multiple correlation coefficient obtained for the cumulative relationship of three cognitive skills with the measure of arts interest (.44) represented a partial replication of the finding reported for 8th graders. The 12th-grade results differed from the earlier finding with respect to the variances attributable to cognitive skills within the same set. Although the 8th-grade value was largely a reflection of the correlation of divergent thinking with arts interest, the 12th-grade value was largely a result of correlations of logical and creative thinking with arts interest. The difference, as noted earlier, may have been a function of the development of logic between 14 and 18 years and of the redesign of the creative-thinking measure to put it on a logical foundation (i.e., uses for objects).

Whatever the cause or causes for the difference, the magnitude of the multiple correlation is significant, particularly in comparison to other attempts to establish correlations between cognitive skills and career interests. One recent attempt (Kelso, Holland, & Gottfredson, 1977) found the largest canonical correlation between the six activity scales of the SDS (corresponding to the six UNIACT scales) and the nine scales of the *Armed Services Vocational Aptitude Battery* to be only .48. A similar correlation calculated in the present study for comparative purposes between the four cognitive skills scores and the six UNIACT scales was somewhat higher (.51). If only four cognitive skills with modest reliability predicted career interests as well as or better than nine highly reliable aptitude scales, aptitude tests not only fail to assess a comprehensive range of human talent (Kelso et al., 1977), they fail to assess a comprehensive range of cognitive skill.

When the focus of the study shifted to the small group of arts-oriented students, the significance of cognitive skills was somewhat diminished. This effect may have resulted from the small size of the arts-oriented group (which made achieving the criterion of significance more difficult) and the separation of cognitive skills for analytical purposes. Even so, it was apparent that arts-oriented students *tended* to be both more logical and more creative in their thinking than did other students. When the results in Table 5.4 are compared with those in Table 4.3, one can see that this tendency was more pronounced in 12th grade than in 8th grade. Still, it appears in both sets of results.

What was surprising in the study of 12th graders was the significantly higher level of insight among arts-oriented students in comparison to other students. The relative significance of this finding in comparison to logic, combined with the relative significance of creative thinking in comparison to divergent thinking, leads to the conclusion that problem finding in a logical mode is a factor related to the arts orientation by 12th grade. These results should be compared with those for 5th graders (Chapter 2), and contrasted with those for 8th graders (Chapter 4).

The results that present the greatest complexity for interpretation are those obtained from testing the third hypothesis, which predicted relationships between cognitive skills and creative behaviors. There are two patterns that overlap in Table 5.3. One, as mentioned, is the correlation of all cognitive skills with achievement in science. The other pattern is the presence of correlations of cognitive skills with achievements in Literature and Art as opposed to Music, Performing Arts, and Crafts. Both patterns seem highly significant. They confirm that cognitive skills are correlated with scientific achievements and selected areas of artistic achievement as early as high school. Put somewhat differently, these results signify that achievements in art and literature are no less strongly associated with logic, divergent thinking, and creative thinking than are achievements in what are commonly considered the more rigorous disciplines of math and science.

These findings were important, and their educational implications will be explored in Chapter 7, but what about music and the performing arts? Why did they not share in the correlations with cognitive skills? Other researchers (e.g., Milgram & Milgram, 1976; Runco, 1986) found similar differences between art and literature on the one hand and music and performing arts on the other. What may begin to explain these differences is the supposition that problem solving does not play a role at all *levels* of artistic performance, even though it may play a role in all domains. In particular, proficiency in music and the performing arts may call for automatization of psychomotor skills more than for adaptation or origination of performances.

Automaticity involves performing in a skilled manner without detailed awareness, freeing the individual to engage in other aspects of the task, such as form and style in music or dance (Schmidt, 1988, p. 74). Origination involves creating new performances (e.g, composing music or choreographing a dance), a higher-order skill than automatization (Simpson, 1972). Responses from subjects to Music and Performing Arts items at the automatic level of performance (e.g., held a recital, had a dramatic role, performed ballet or modern dance in a show or contest) seemed to outweigh responses at the adaptive or original levels, resulting in diminished correlations between thinking skills and these domains of creative behaviors.

This explanation is supported by the discovery that among the small group of arts-oriented seniors, achievements in music and the performing arts were significantly greater than similar achievements among other students. In other words, when the importance of thinking skills was diminished by adopting an interest or personality approach rather than a cognitive approach to creativity, the relationship between the arts orientation and both music and the performing arts emerged, as one might expect from the correlations in Table 5.1. When viewed from a cognitive perspective, the expected relationship between creativity and musical or dramatic arts achievements disappears, suggesting that musical and dramatic achievements are not based on cognitive skills at the high school level of performance.

There is some evidence of a third pattern of correlations in Table 5.3, but it offers a continuing challenge to improve measures of cognitive skill. The different correlations of creative and divergent thinking with Literature, Art, and Math-Science can largely be attributed to the different reliabilities of the two cognitive skills tests. The correlations of divergent thinking and creative thinking with crafts are too different to be explained in this manner, but the difference appears to be related to the nature of crafts, which do not require problem finding.

Still, creative- and divergent-thinking skills were not well distinguished from each other by the tests designed to measure them. Creative thinking has over the course of several studies (Chapters 2 and 4) appeared to be highly dependent on divergent thinking for the task to be invented.

When added to divergent thinking in this study, problem finding did seem to weaken the relationships between divergent thinking and technical interests, and divergent thinking and production of crafts. It also seemed to strengthen the relationship of divergent thinking to arts interest. Work needs to continue, however, on a method to assess creative thinking that is not as dependent on divergent thinking as was the creative-thinking measure used in this study.

Perhaps the most important conclusion that could be reached from this study of cognitive skills in relation to the arts orientation is that *by 12th grade, creative thinking is a farily well-established blend of cognitive skills, including logic, divergent thinking, and problem finding.* This "blend" lends more meaning to the definition of creative thinking offered in Chapter 2 —meaningful response to conditions that call for finding a problem and solving it in one's own way. One may conclude from the study of creative thinking among high school seniors that when a problem requires a logically meaningful but not necessarily "correct" solution, logic as well as intuition is required to find a problem and then solve it. Logic appears to be a prerequisite, both developmentally and ontologically, to adult creative thinking. One must know what logical problems are and how to solve them before one can profitably set out to find them.

*   *   *

The consistent finding—across different age levels, measures, and methods of investigation—that cognitive skills are correlated with interest in and orientation toward the arts seems to reflect a relationship that has implications for arts curricula. Previous studies, reviewed in Chapter 1, have discovered different dimensions of the cognition-arts relationship, but few if any have surveyed the general relationship and followed through with implications for education in the arts. Before exploring the educational implications, however, one more study needs to be reported that is highly suggestive of future research.

chapter 6
Stories for the Thematic Apperception Test Blank Card

The *Thematic Apperception Test* (TAT; Murray, 1943) begins with the examiner telling the examinee that "this is a test of imagination, one form of intelligence" (p. 3). The examinee is then told that he or she will be shown some pictures, one at a time, and "your task will be to make up as dramatic a story as you can for each" (1943, p. 3). Although the test is purportedly of imagination, its real purpose is to reveal some of the "drives, emotions, sentiments, complexes and conflicts of a personality" (p. 1). Imagination or the "momentary creativity" of the subject was designed as the means, not the end, of the TAT technique.

When in 1946, Anne Roe looked for evidence of the creativity of male artists in their TAT stories, she and others were generally discouraged by the findings (Bellak, 1958; Burchard, 1952). Little evidence other than "an additional unusual twist here and there" in the stories was obtained to indicate the special talents of the 18 examinees. In fact, "they were, without exception so appalled by the poor quality of the pictures, artistically speaking, that they had repeatedly to be recalled from critical comments to the task at hand" (Roe, 1946b, p. 405).

Murray had without explanation included a blank card (No. 16) in the final version of the complete TAT set. Although Roe used different cards with different examinees, a table of her results (Roe, 1946a) reveals that these included Cards 1–11, 13, and 14. Later, when the set became standardized for her famous work with scientists (Roe, 1953), 10 cards from the first 15 in the TAT set were used, but not the last five cards, including Card 16. Card 16 would have given the subject an opportunity to "see what you can see on this blank card. Imagine some picture there and describe it to me in detail....Now tell me a story about it" (Murray, 1943, p. 5).

Card 16 might have been the only one to appeal to artists, because it would have been the only one to allow them to find a problem (Getzels & Csikszentmihalyi, 1976) before solving it expressively. The blank card would have allowed artists to set a problem rather than respond to the presented ones represented by the picture cards. The unanimity of the artists' critical comments suggests that they were engaging in art criticism—thinking evaluatively—rather than being expressive or creative. To release their creative energies in more than "an unusual twist here and there," the card before them would had to have been blank, like an empty canvas.

One of the earliest comments about the blank card was that it represented "a testing of limits" (Tomkins, 1947, p. 23). Similarly, Henry (1956) observed of the blank card that its value lay "in the extreme challenge which it makes for the subject who must create for himself the entire scene as well as its people, events, and plot development" (p. 46). According to Bellak (1986), this characteristic makes the blank card

> of extreme value with verbally gifted subjects, who may really let loose and project freely. If the subject has given previous indications that he has difficulty in expressing fantasy material, however, the blank card is often of no value. (p. 62)

Bellak recounted an experience testing engineering students and English majors, which made an impression "to the extent that I almost categorically speak of subjects giving meager stories as engineers and of those with lively imaginations as English majors" (p. 62). The problem for creativity researchers lies in determining to what extent lengthy responses to this card represent creative thinking apart from verbal ability or facility.

Despite the many studies of creativity in the 1960s and 1970s that used cards from the TAT, none reported results for the blank card (No. 16). This fact motivated a research project in which the focus was on the relationship between responses to the blank card of the TAT and scores on traditional measures of creative thinking (Wakefield, 1986). Although these results will be summarized first, additional analysis of blank card stories in light of college students' career choices may provide even greater insight into the nature of creative thinking. This analysis, which sorts the stories by college major but which maintains a quantitative perspective, will be presented second. Finally, the content of blank card stories by fine arts majors will be analyzed for themes which reveal insights about the motivation or personality of arts students.

The hypotheses of the initial study were simple. It was expected that:

1. Total wordage of subjects in response to the blank card should correlate positively with creative-thinking test scores, and
2. That wordage would correlate with test scores more highly for the blank card than for picture cards.

If supported, these hypotheses would suggest that response to the blank card is the product of creative thought and might be useful for closer study of creative thinking.

THE EMPIRICAL INVESTIGATION

Participants were recruited from students in an undergraduate educational psychology course at a large but highly selective university. Of a total of 74 participants, 59 satisfied the criteria of (a) attend both testing sessions, (b) be native English speaking, and (c) agree to let responses be tape recorded. Many of the subjects were in preteaching or prenursing programs, but their primary affiliations were with diverse colleges of the university. Of the 47 female participants, 6 were from the college of agriculture, 7 from applied life sciences, 5 from fine and applied arts, 25 from liberal arts and sciences, 1 each from three other colleges (nursing, communications, and the graduate college), and 1 nondegree student. Of the 12 male participants, 4 were from applied life sciences, 6 were from liberal arts and sciences, and 1 each was from engineering and fine and applied arts. Even if most of the students were in teacher education or prenursing programs, and even though females heavily outnumbered males, the students represented a good cross-section of the colleges on campus. Most of the female subjects were sophomores (43%) or juniors (30%), and most of the male subjects were juniors (42%) or seniors (42%). The average age of females was 20 years and 11 months ($SD = 1.8$ years), and the average age of males was 21 years and 6 months ($SD = 1.0$ years).

Three instruments were used in the study. The version of the TAT that was used differed for females and males. Female subjects were administered (in this order) Cards 1, 2, 4, 7GF (Girl/Female), 9GF, 10, 13MF (Male/Female), 14, 16(blank), and 18GF. Card 1, for example, is described as a young boy contemplating "a violin which rests on a table in front of him" (Murray, 1943, p. 18). Male subjects were administered the same cards, except corresponding cards from the "Boy/Male" series were substituted for 7GF, 9GF, and 18GF. In either case, 10 TAT cards formed the principal instrument of this study. Total wordage in response to each card (with the exception of questions to the examiner) was used as the principal measure.

Given that a continuous flow of words was desired as a measure of responsiveness, the standard instructions for the blank card were modified slightly so that the examiner would not have to interrupt the response with the instruction, "Now tell me a story about it." The instructions for this study were "see what you can see on this blank card. Imagine some picture there and describe it to me in detail, *then tell me a story about it.*" This modification, to allow for uninterrupted instructions by the examiner followed by an uninterrupted response by the examinee, was the only alteration from the standard instructions for administering this instrument.

The tests used as measures of cognitive skills related to creative thinking included the *Remote Associates Test* (RAT; College/Adult, Form 1) and Unusual Uses from the *Torrance Tests of Creative Thinking* (TTCT; Form B). The RAT is based on an associative interpretation of the creative process (Mednick & Mednick, 1967). Subjects are required to complete each item with a word from three low probability (or remote) associates of that word. (For example, rat: blue: cottage: _____.) The RAT score has been found to be associated with verbal ability as well as creativity (Hargreaves & Bolton, 1972). Subjects were given 33 minutes rather than the usual 40 to finish this 30-item test. The split-half reliability estimate was .78.

The RAT was also used to control for contamination of responses to the TAT by verbosity, glibness, or other forms of verbal response that might lack meaningfulness. Because the number of associates for a given word or syllable can be considered a measure of its meaningfulness (Noble, 1952; Klatzky, 1980, p. 219), and because each associate in an item stem may be considered a partial meaning of the correct answer (Mednick, 1976), then by definition each incorrect response on the RAT might be considered less meaningful than a correct response. Because examinees are not required to answer all of the RAT items, and in fact almost never do, the ratio of correct to total written responses might be considered a measure of the overall *economy* of response. Such a measure could be correlated with wordage to control for possible contamination. The split-half reliability estimate of this economy index was also .78.

Unusual Uses from the TTCT (Torrance, 1974a) is a divergent-thinking test that calls for the subject to generate as many uses as possible for the specified object in 10 minutes. Responses were scored for fluency, flexibility, and originality by two self-trained scorers. The split-half interscorer reliability estimates were .99, .86, and .96. No estimate of test response reliability could be calculated from the data in this study, but Yamamoto (cited in Torrance, 1965) found retest reliabilities over 10 weeks for fluency, flexibility, and originality scores on this exercise to be .75, .60, and .64.

Table 6.1. Means and Standard Deviations for Female College Students ($N=47$)

Variable	Mean	SD
Wordage of Response		
TAT Pictures	226.0	114.0
Blank Card	273.0	208.0
RAT Scores		
Correct	13.2	5.3
Error	7.4	5.6
Unusual Uses Scores		
Fluency	21.0	8.1
Flexibility	11.4	3.2
Originality	25.2	10.8

Two 50-minute testing sessions were scheduled, one for small group testing and the other for individually administering the TAT. The subjects in the small group sessions were given a general orientation using the TTCT instructions as a model, and then subjects were administered Unusual Uses. This exercise was followed by the RAT. Within a week of group testing, the TAT was individually administered according to standard instructions, with the minor exception explained above. Because responses were to be tape recorded, subjects were asked if it was acceptable if their anonymous responses were recorded. All but one participant agreed to let their responses be recorded. That single data set was not included in the study.

Responses to the tests were correlated and correlational values were compared to test hypothesized differences, then responses to the blank card were contrasted with responses to picture cards for subjects categorized by their major fields of study. A "creativity index" was calculated using a ratio of blank card to average picture card wordage for individuals in different academic majors. Finally, the responses to the blank card by the 6 fine arts majors (5 females and 1 male) were chosen for closer study.

Statistical Results

Because different TAT cards were used for females and males, and because the two groups were disproportionate in size, the statistical results were separated. Those for the female subjects will be presented first.

Table 6.1 presents the means and standard deviations of variables for the female subjects. What seemed especially interesting about wordage of response to the blank card was its high standard deviation when compared with wordage of response to picture cards. When the distribution of blank card responses was plotted against the distribution of picture

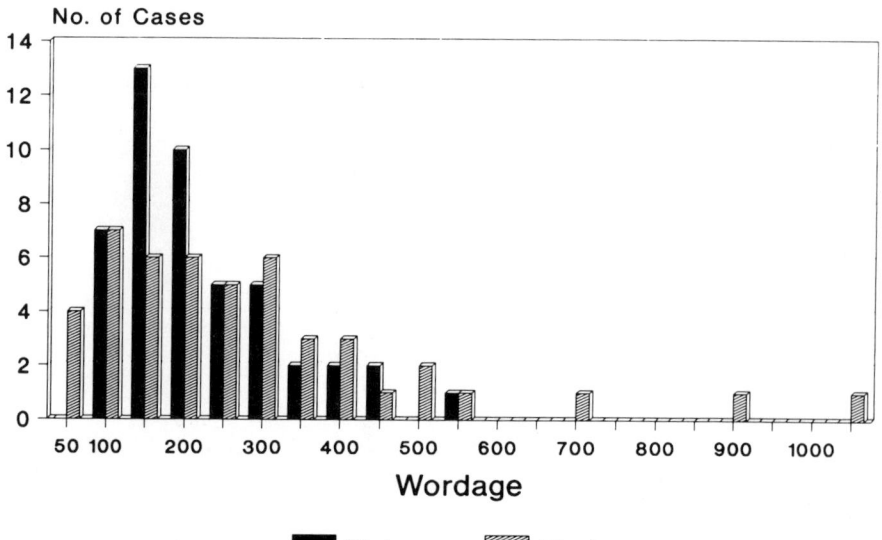

Figure 6.1. Distribution of blank card response wordage for females.

card responses, it was clear that blank card responses had greater positive skew (see Figure 6.1), with a few extremely high responses.

Several of the statistical hypotheses were generally confirmed for the female subjects. Although none of the correlations between response wordage to individual TAT cards and Unusual Uses fluency and flexibility scores were significant, the correlations between wordage of response to Card 16 (the blank card) and the Unusual Uses fluency score tended to be positive (.23, n.s.). Correlations of response wordage to Cards 14 and 16 and the Unusual Uses originality score were significant (.27, $p < .05$). Card 14 is especially interesting because somewhat like the blank card, the subject must imagine most of the picture. Murray (1943) described Card 14 as "the silhouette of a man (or woman) against a bright window. The rest of the picture is totally black" (p. 20). The degree of significance of this pair of correlational values was perhaps not as important as their uniqueness among 30 coefficients (3 coefficients for each of 10 TAT cards).

Correlations of wordage with RAT scores were more often significant, perhaps because of the relationship of the RAT to verbal ability. Values for Cards 1 (.35, $p < .01$), 13MF (.32, $p < .05$), and 16 (.34, $p < .01$) all reached significant levels. Card 1 has already been described. Card 13MF portrays a man standing in front of a partially clothed woman lying in bed. Why the RAT score should be correlated with responses to Cards 1 and 13MF is uncertain, but response to only the blank card correlated

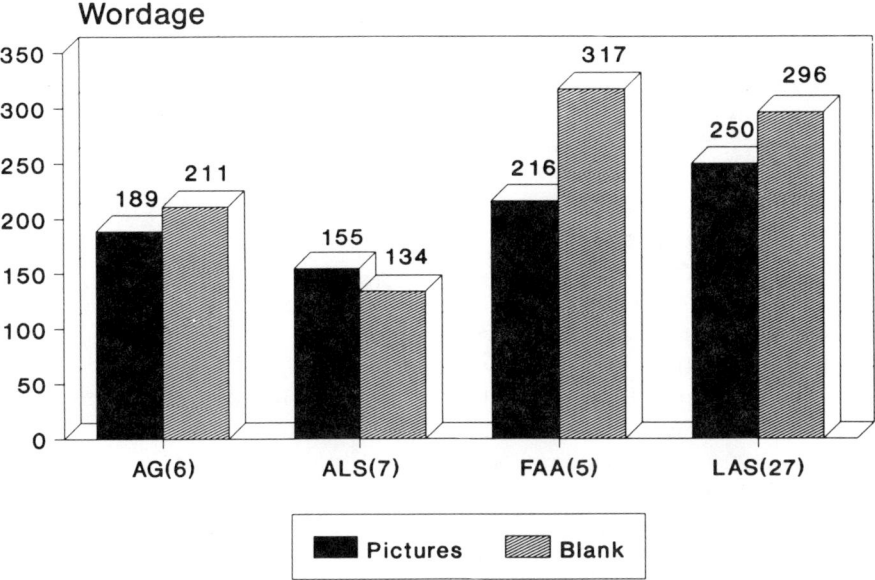

Figure 6.2. Average blank card response lengths for females by college.

positively and significantly with scores on both the divergent-thinking test and the RAT.

The second hypothesis was pursued by testing for differences between correlations for the blank card and corresponding correlations for the picture cards. The blank card correlations were significantly higher than picture card correlations in 12 out of 36 cases, including at least once for every Unusual Uses or RAT variable, and at least once for seven out of nine picture cards. Cards 1 and 14 were the exceptions.

When the "economy index" from the RAT was correlated with wordage of response to each of the 10 cards, significantly positive results were found for responses to Cards 1 (.36, $p < .01$), 13MF (.35, $p < .01$), 14 (.29, $p < .05$), and 16 (.41, $p < .01$). The blank card value was higher than the values for five of the six remaining picture cards. Although not entirely independent of the other results, these findings provided some evidence that the blank card not only stimulated creative thinking, but it inhibited glib, insincere, or otherwise less than meaningful responses among the female subjects.

TAT responses were sorted by academic major to gain some insight into the relationship between the responses to the two different types of TAT card (picture or blank) and the subject's field of study. Figure 6.2 portrays the female TAT responses divided among the four colleges that were significantly represented: agriculture (AG); applied life sciences

(ALS); fine and applied arts (FAA); and liberal arts and sciences (LAS), including the graduate chemistry student and the nondegree student. These labels lie alphabetically arrayed along the horizontal of Figure 6.2. The vertical represents wordage in response to the nine picture cards (black bars) and in response to the blank card (lightly shaded bars). Average values are at the top of each bar.

What is striking about Figure 6.2 is the ranking of the groups. The fine and applied arts majors (in art and in music) were more responsive to the blank card than were arts and sciences majors; arts and sciences majors were more responsive than agriculture majors; and agriculture majors were more responsive than applied life sciences majors. Figure 6.3 further breaks down the results for the arts and sciences majors, a group much larger than the rest. The 10 arts students (LAS-Arts) were largely from language arts, including foreign-language teachers in training. The 12 science students (LAS-Sci) included majors in mathematics as well as those majoring in biology, chemistry, psychology, and linguistics. Nine of the 10 general curriculum students (LAS-Gen) were in a prenursing curriculum. Notice again that the ranking of majors in terms of their responsiveness to the blank card proceeded from liberal arts or humanities majors to science majors, and from science majors to the general curriculum students (mostly prenursing). One should also observe, however, that responsiveness to the picture cards seems to follow the same ranking as responsiveness to the blank card, suggesting a need to control for verbal ability or facility in response to the tasks.

Recall that to control for the variance in length of responses to all cards, a "creativity index" was devised as the ratio of blank card to picture card wordage. Table 6.2 presents the results of calculating this index for the data presented in Figures 6.2 and 6.3. The general conclusion that can be reached from Table 6.2 is that the ranking of majors which is depicted in the figures tends to be preserved when verbal ability or facility is controlled. Fine arts teachers in training were more differentially responsive to the blank card than were arts and sciences teachers in training, and so on down the list of colleges and majors. Responsiveness to the blank card appears to have been an even better indication of an arts orientation—and perhaps creativity—than was performance on either cognitive skill test.

The results for two female subjects who were not affiliated with one of the four principal subgroups were treated separately. These subjects were from the college of communications (an advertising major) and the college of nursing. The length of the communication student's response to the blank card was 331 words, and the average length of her responses to the nine picture cards was 243, resulting in a creativity index of 1.36.

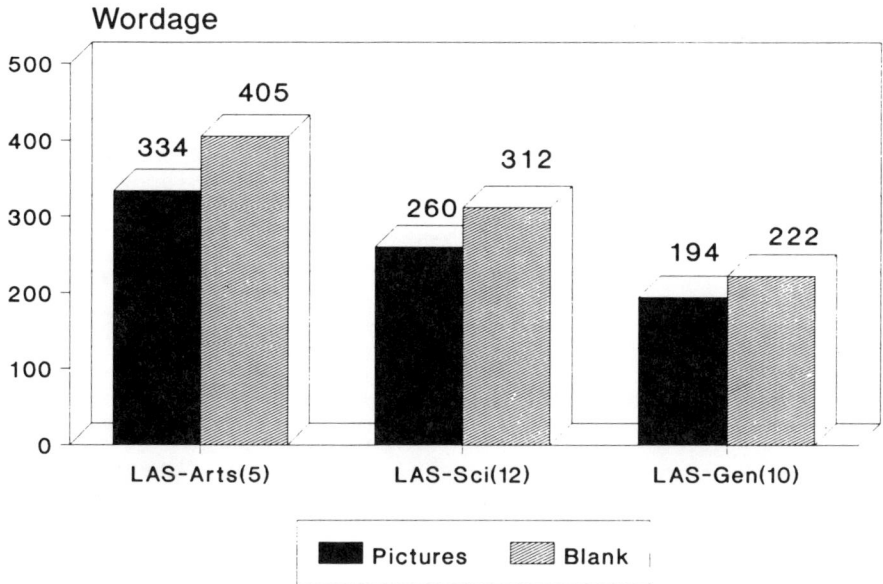

Figure 6.3. Average blank card response lengths for female LAS students by major.

Table 6.2. Creativity Indices* of Female College Students (N=45)

College Affiliation	N		Creativity Index	
Fine and Applied Arts	5			1.37
Music	3		1.47	
Art	2		1.23	
Liberal Arts and Sciences	27			1.18
Arts	5		1.20	
Sciences	12		1.20	
General	10		1.16	
Agriculture	6			1.04
Institutional Management	1		1.54	
Dietetics	3		.98	
Home Economics	2		.89	
Applied Life Sciences	7			.88
Health	3		1.04	
Physical Education	4		.76	
Total or Average	45	45		1.12

*Wordage in response to the blank card divided by average wordage in response to nine picture cards. Values represent average indices for individuals in each category.

Table 6.3. Means and Standard Deviations for Male College Students ($N=12$)

Variable	Mean	SD
Wordage of Response		
TAT Pictures	218.0	85.0
Blank Card	286.0	175.0
RAT Scores		
Correct	14.8	3.0
Error	5.2	2.7
Unusual Uses Scores		
Fluency	15.0	7.8
Flexibility	9.5	3.0
Originality	18.4	7.8

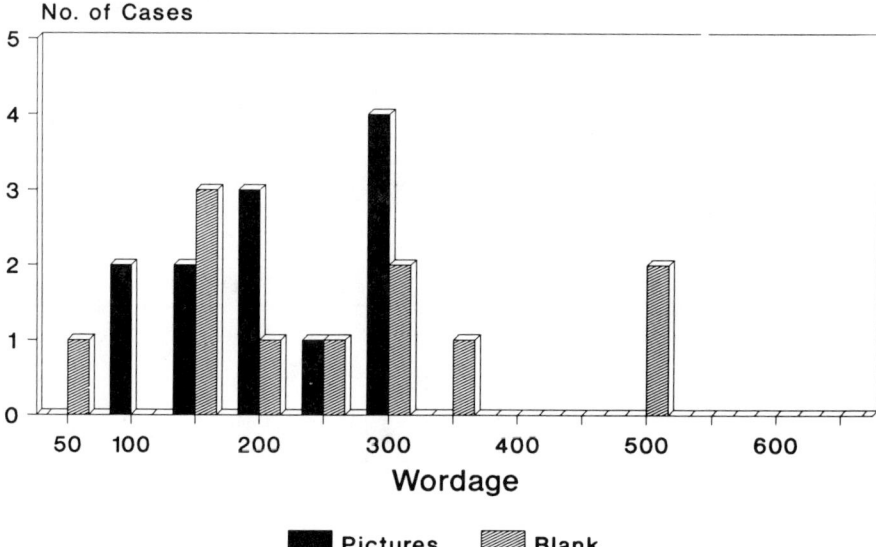

Figure 6.4. Distribution of blank card response wordage for males.

This value was higher than the average for arts and sciences students but lower than that for fine arts students. The length of the nursing student's response to the blank card was 697 words, and the average length of her responses to the picture cards was 335, resulting in a creativity index of 2.08. This value was above the fine arts average.

Table 6.3 presents the means and standard deviations of study measures for men. Like the average wordage of blank card responses by females, average blank card wordage for males was accompanied by a relatively high standard deviation. Figure 6.4 plots the distributions of blank card and picture card responses, and a similar pattern to that for

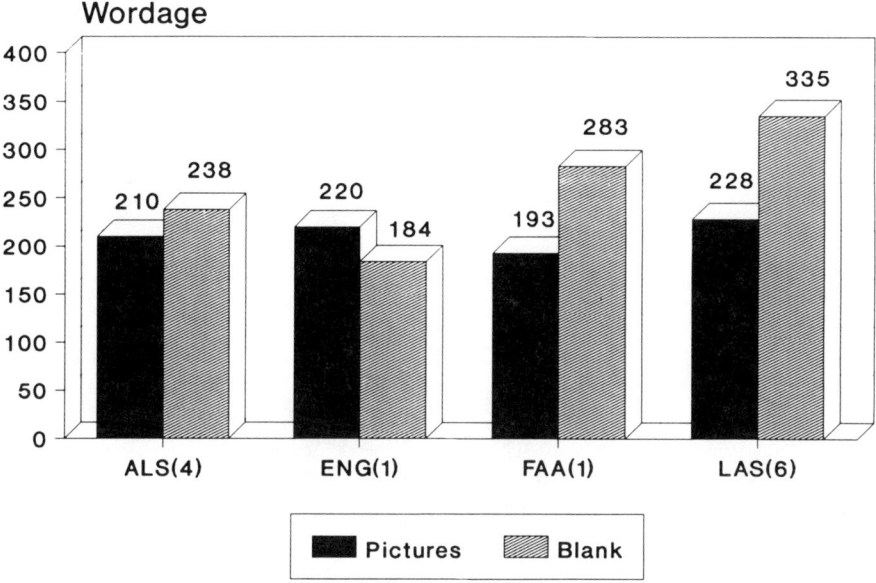

Figure 6.5. Average blank card response lengths for males by college.

the female subjects appeared. Blank card responses appeared to be more variable than picture card responses because they were more highly skewed.

The results of correlating TAT response wordage with cognitive skills test scores for the small group of male subjects were more problematic. None of the correlational values reached significance. Even the pattern in the results for female subjects disappeared. Neither were economy indices of the male subjects positively correlated with response wordage for the blank card or other cards, suggesting that responses to the TAT cards for this group were not as meaningful as corresponding responses for the female subjects.

When TAT responses for male subjects were sorted by major, however, a familiar pattern appeared (Figure 6.5). Subjects who were more responsive to the blank card tended to be from the fine arts or the liberal arts and sciences, and those who were less responsive were from applied life sciences or engineering. Although picture card responses from the four groups were approximately equal in length, calculation of a creativity index for each group resulted in confirmation of the pattern in Figure 6.5. The highest creativity index belonged to the lone fine arts student (1.47), a music major. The next highest creativity index belonged to the group of arts and science students (1.33), including science majors and one general curriculum (undecided) major. The next to lowest creativity

Table 6.4. Means and Standard Deviations for Fine Arts Majors ($N=6$)

Variable	Mean	SD
Wordage of Response		
TAT Pictures	212.0	67.0
Blank Card	312.0	185.0
RAT Scores		
Correct	13.2	5.2
Error	7.2	3.9
Unusual Uses Scores		
Fluency	22.5	3.3
Flexibility	11.4	1.8
Originality	26.9	9.5

index belonged to the group of applied life sciences students (1.04), mostly physical education majors. The lowest creativity index belonged to the single engineering student (.84), who was majoring in computer science. These indices seemed to correspond quite well with similar calculations for female subjects (Table 6.2). Overall, both female and male fine arts students had the highest creativity indices.

Case Study Results

Case data for six fine arts students (five female and one male) are presented in Appendix B. These cases were chosen because the students had clearly chosen artistic careers, even if the careers were within school settings. Table 6.4 summarizes the numerical data for the group. When these data are visually compared with the data in Table 6.1, the means of the test scores of the fine arts students appear to be almost identical to similar means for the 47 female subjects. Further, although the fine arts mean for Unusual Uses scores surpassed the corresponding mean for male subjects (Table 6.3), the male subject mean for the RAT surpassed that of the fine arts students. Given that five of the six fine arts students were female, and given that test scores for the fine arts students were neither consistently above nor below corresponding means for male subjects, the cognitive skills test scores could not be said to differentiate this group from the norms.

The measurable differences between the fine arts group and the norm groups lay in the average length of response to the blank card. Although the mean of the picture card responses for the fine arts group was very similar to corresponding means for the females and males in the norm groups (represented in Tables 6.1 and 6.3), the mean of the blank card response for the fine arts group (312 words) was higher than corresponding means for both females (273 words) and males (286 words). Blank card stories by fine arts students were on average 10 percent to 15 percent longer than the study norms. Because the fine arts students were included in the norm groups, the differences between the fine arts mean and the means of nonarts groups would have been somewhat greater, but still would not have been statistically significant.

The significance of the responses by fine arts students to the blank card lies not only in wordage, but in response content. At this point, the reader is encouraged to read the blank card responses of these six individuals in Appendix B. The following discussion will assume knowledge of these responses, and will refer to blank card descriptions and stories without lengthy quotations.

Characterizing the blank card responses of the fine arts students as a group was not easy. Despite their unusual average length, they had a high variance (as indicated in Table 6.4). Only two of the six blank card responses by fine arts subjects were among the six longest blank card stories. The longest stories in the study came from diverse sources: a student majoring in psychology, a male student in the general curriculum (undecided), a nursing student, a graduate student in chemistry, and the two fine arts majors (one art and one music major).

At one extreme of the fine arts responses was a very short description that fixed on an image of a cloud and trailed off into an ambiguous ending (Case 70). This type of response was common among the shortest ones in the study, most of which echoed the whiteness of the blank card. Here the echo was the image of a cloud through which a character, carried by "Zeus or something," was ascending. The "whiteness" of the central image indicated the essentially stimulus-bound nature of the response. When perception was stimulus-bound, but when there was nothing to bind to except the blank, the result was an image that echoed the blank and no story.

At the other extreme was a long, replete, and dynamic description of a landscape with a town, seen from an aerial view (Case 1). The description contained several unusual twists, such as the dragon outside the town, who "isn't as bad as he likes to make everyone feel, but he just keeps everyone on their toes." Absent from this imagined picture were "story things that have just castles and stuff." The description was not stereotypical, but neither did the harmonious scene suggest a story. No problem was perceived. Like Case 70, Case 1 failed to find a problem to motivate the development of a plot.

The other four responses by fine arts students to the blank card all developed stories. The stimulus properties of the blank card could be perceived in some of these stories, although in others, they could not. In the story of the secret pet (Case 24), for example, the task of the blank card apparently evoked a story on the basis of not knowing "what to say"—the feeling that the little girl had when her mother confronted her about the dog in their basement. A response based on a feeling was more clearly evident in the story about the desert traveler (Case 33). The mention of desert, loss of materials, "flat sand," barrenness, and emptiness were all related to the perception of a blank card, but perception was not stimulus-bound.

Possibilities were intuited in the "barrenness" through the projection of an affective landscape. The feelings "that had always been there in his life regardless of the barrenness" became the source of a story. Metaphorically, they were equated with "sagebrush and other desert plants" before they were transformed into unelaborated abilities and dreams, and then disappeared. The subject called on his internal resources in response to the blank card, and the result was a quite creative story.

The other two responses deserve to be interpreted simultaneously. They differed greatly in length—one less than 150 words and the other over 500 words—and they differed greatly in creativity indices (.57 vs. 1.98), but they possessed other characteristics which were similar. First, both the brief description of the green cat (Case 53) and the detailed portrayal of a landscape "in the pioneer days" (Case 50) contained vivid imagery, including color. The cat is not just green, it is a "long-haired" green cat. The grass in the landscape is not just green, but a "very bright" green. The color imagery was somewhat remarkable because all of the TAT pictures were black and white.

Second, both stories were essentially concerned with what is original as opposed to conventional or "normal" (the word used by both subjects). The cat, pictured sitting in a window contemplating his "fifth life," had "always been a normal cat until now." This state resulted in the problem which motivated the brief story—"nobody would have him because he was green," but a woman took him in, and "now he's found a home." The child who was the central character in the other story was also exceptional. This child, who "is just an infant," found magic in the woods where his parents were asleep. His mind became advanced, he talked to the animals, and they talked to him before he ended "his little exploration trip" and grew up "like any other normal child." Both of these accounts—of what it is like to be normal in all respects but one—can be said to contain the theme of creative giftedness.

The central figures resembled each other in other details: They possessed their special characteristic by accident; they were independent; they were alone but not lonely; and they seemed to accept themselves for what they were, despite their difference from others. Their difference lay in their originality—who ever heard of a green cat or a child who could talk to animals? Other cats and other children simply did not have the same experience. The differentiating characteristics of each of the central figures are originality and imagination, which make these stories stand out from the rest (except perhaps for the "delusions" and "dreams" of the desert traveler). The theme of creative giftedness in these two stories is not subtle. It is the central theme.

DISCUSSION

The role of this TAT study in relation to earlier studies was both general and specific. The general role was to explore new creativity measures in relation to well-established measures such as the RAT and Unusual Uses from the TTCT. The specific role was to explore creative thinking in greater fullness than allowed by most measures of cognitive skills.

Departing from earlier studies, this research focused on blank card response length as an indication of creative thinking. Correlations of wordage of response to the blank card with cognitive skills traditionally associated with creative thinking were positive but moderate (between .25 and .35). No similar pattern of correlations was found between cognitive skills scores and wordages in response to nine picture cards. These findings suggest that there is a relationship between responsiveness to the blank card and creative thinking, as creative thinking has been traditionally conceived.

When the distributions of blank card and picture card responses were charted, they clearly revealed differences between the two types of responses for both female and male subjects (Figures 6.1 and 6.4). Picture card stories were distributed for both groups in a comparatively narrow range. Blank card responses were more variable, particularly at the upper extreme. The extremely lengthy responses tended to come from individuals with very high creativity indices. These subjects seemed to "let loose" in response to the blank card in comparison to their own responses to picture cards. These distributions raise the possibility that creative thinking may not be normally distributed. In measurement terms, the curve may be "positively skewed." Although the assumption of a normal distribution is psychometrically convenient, and is an essential assumption for correlational studies (Cohen & Cohen, 1975), the assumption of normality in the distribution may not be realistic for creative thinking. The comparison of intelligence and creative thinking might more appropriately involve the comparison of a bell-shaped curve with a highly skewed distribution.

Because of the possibility that verbal contaminants might be partly responsible for wordage, a number of precautions were taken to control for the accidental effects of verbal facility. First, an economy index was developed as a ratio of meaningful to total responses on the RAT. This ratio proved to be reliable, and for females was significantly correlated with blank card responses. Responses by female subjects could be said to be economical or meaningful in response to the task. Second, a creativity index was devised as a ratio of blank card to picture card wordage to control for verbal ability in response to the TAT. This creativity index, which did not alter the distribution of blank card responses (see Chapter 7), was used in subsequent analyses rather than blank card wordage.

These analyses included a reasonable estimate of the rankings of fields of study or vocations by the extent of their association with creative thinking, as determined by the creativity index. The rankings of these areas would be: first, the fine arts; second, the liberal arts and sciences; third, technical vocations (e.g., dieticians, home economists, nurses); and fourth, applied life sciences. Not enough subjects from communications or engineering colleges were administered the TAT to include these areas in the rankings. Subfields could be ranked within major areas, but the weakness of this approach was brought out when these smaller units proved to have higher or lower creativity indices than neighboring vocational areas. The weakness of the small group approach was easily apparent when individual respondents within each smaller unit (such as music and art) were found with a creativity index higher or lower than the group index for *any* area.

As a consequence, four out of the six students who gave the longest responses to the blank card, and who had the highest creativity indices, were found to be students majoring in something other than fine arts. This finding raised a question about the usefulness of ranking vocational areas by their creativity indices when within-group variation was as great as, if not greater than, between-group variation. This finding also raised a question about the accuracy of the creativity index as a measure suitable for individual identification of talent.

Neither of these questions could be answered by the data collected for this study. Instead, the focus of the study shifted to the blank card responses by the fine arts students. This focus permitted closer analysis of the responses of an artistically oriented group than possible in previous chapters.

The visual and auditory talents of art and music students could not be expected to show up on tests which require only verbal response, and indeed they did not. The overall mean test scores of the fine arts group did not differ from the norms. What is surprising is that the creative talents of this group were apparent in wordage for the blank card and in the creativity index, indicating that response was more than verbal, drawing on conative and affective elements that go into creative thinking (e.g., Amabile, 1985; Csikszentmihalyi & Getzels, 1988; Maddi, 1975). The blank card provided the subjects the opportunity to find a problem, possibly making response to it a more sensitive measure of creativity than was performance on either cognitive skill test.

The focus of the study finally shifted to what the content of blank card stories might reveal about the motivation or personality of fine arts students. Two discoveries are relevant here. First, finding a problem to solve apparently motivated the development of a plot. Logic was represented in the development of a plot, or a working out of the solution to the problem that the subject had found. In this respect, the responses of fine arts students were not unique. When a subject failed to find a problem, no matter how elaborate the development of the imaginary scene, no story developed. The story was the logically related solution to the problem. Even among the fine arts group, the longer responses to the blank card tended to be the ones which included the best problems to solve.

The second discovery was suggested by the special content of two of the six stories by the fine arts students. These two stories seemed to contain themes of creative giftedness—what it is like to be exceptionally creative. Although the test scores and even wordage of blank card stories did not validate that both of these individuals were creative, their fields of study (art and music) were creative, and their creative themes may have future value for hypotheses about the self-perceptions of creative individuals.

Such creative individuals may perceive themselves to differ from social norms in a single respect, rather than multiple respects. Their self-perception seems to be of a person whose difference may not be perceived by others because of otherwise normal characteristics, or if perceived, might be rejected by others because of its abnormalcy. Their one exceptionality appears to be central to their view of themselves, and the relation between this exceptionality and the norm appears to be a source of contemplation.

chapter 7
Theoretical and Educational Implications

This chapter begins with an observation made by Rosenzweig and Fleming (1949), who compiled norms for the TAT cards—including reaction time, total wordage, and response duration—shortly after the TAT was published. They wrote:

> The general observation should be made with respect to all three quantitative measures discussed in this section that the responses to Card 16 (blank card) stand out for both men and women as noticably deviant from those for the other cards. The variability of the means is especially great. These facts should be recalled in the interpretation of any quantitative deviations found for this card. (p. 500)

The data presented in Chapter 6 convey the impression that blank card responses are highly variable because they are positively skewed. Figure 6.1 in particular revealed that a few extreme responses led to a distribution with a long "tail" on the right side which sloped gently in comparison to the left side of the curve, which was rather steep. What theoretical significance might this observation have for understanding creative thinking?

This chapter reviews the evidence presented throughout earlier chapters and by other studies to determine if skew is characteristic of distributions of response to different exercises which call for finding a problem and solving it in one's own way. An interpretation will then be offered for the significance of skew in light of various characterizations of creative thinking and creativity. Later in the chapter, the educational

Table 7.1. Cross-Study Comparisons of Creative Thinking

Open Stimulus	Source	Age S	N	Mean	SD
Timed Tests					
Shapes and Lines	Chapter 4	14	74	31.1	15.5
Uses for Objects	Wakefield (1989)	18	65	21.7	8.4
Untimed Tests					
Patterns and Lines	Chapter 2	11	23	4.8	2.7
Discovered Items	Runco & Okuda (1988)				
Uses for Objects		16–18	29	17.9	9.9
Instances		16–18	29	25.3	13.6
Similarities		16–18	29	13.9	6.4
TAT Blank Card	Chapter 6				
College Female		20	47	273	208
College Male		21	12	286	185
TAT Blank Card	Rosenzweig & Fleming (1949)				
Female Adult		—	50	166	111
Male Adult		—	50	159	123

implications of the findings from the studies presented in earlier chapters are explored, particularly in relation to cognitive skills training in the arts.

THE DISTRIBUTION OF CREATIVE THINKING

In general, normally distributed responses exist within a relatively narrow range, that is, they are not highly variable in relation to the mean or average. In a normal distribution, 68 percent of responses lie within one standard deviation of the mean, 34 percent above it and 34 percent below it. Approximately 96 percent of responses lie within two standard deviations above and below the mean. Sometimes the normalcy of a distribution of data can be estimated by looking at the mean in relation to the standard deviation.

Table 7.1 displays the means and standard deviations obtained from the measures of creative thinking developed in the course of studies presented over the last five chapters. Along with these results are the means and standard deviations of three measures of response to discovered divergent-thinking items (Runco & Okuda, 1988) and the blank card wordage norms for adult men and women (Rosenzweig & Fleming, 1949). All of these data sources measured responses to items that fit the definition of creative thinking that was presented in Chapter 2. The tasks called for finding a problem and then solving it in one's own way.

In general, the timed tests offer a good possibility of normally distributed responses. Two standard deviations are possible, both above

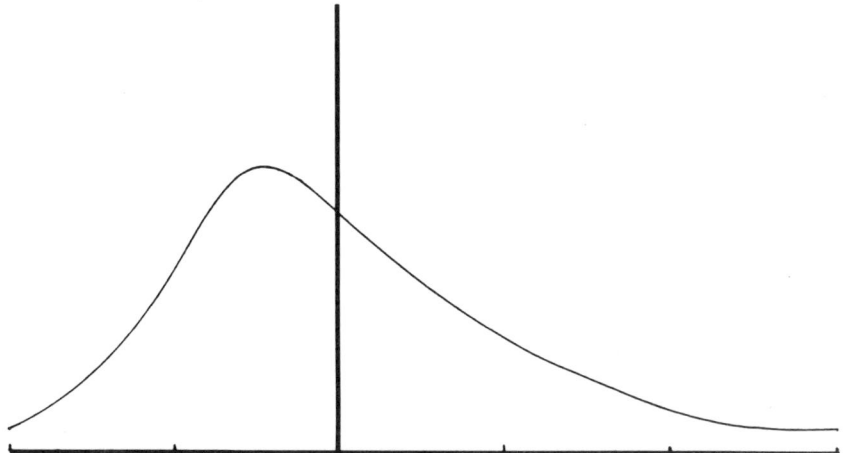

Figure 7.1. Frequency distribution of creativity indices.

and below the norms. The means and standard deviations of the untimed test responses, however, do not allow for two standard deviations below the means, signaling that more variability lay in responses above the means than below them. The characteristic of all such distributions would be positive skew.

If one examines the results in earlier chapters, one must also conclude that the untimed creative-thinking measures (Chapters 2 and 6) were more valid than the timed creative-thinking measures, which were not much more valid than accompanying divergent-thinking exercises. The association between positive skew and the validity of the creative-thinking measures suggests that creative thinking in general may be distributed with the characteristics of positive skew.

The distribution of creative thinking may be likened to the distribu- of creativity indices from the study reported in Chapter 6. This distribution is portrayed in Figure 7.1. The mean or average of these indices is represented by the vertical line. The modal—or most common—response is represented by the top of the curve. Standard deviations are marked off on the horizontal line. In a normal distribution, the mean would lie at the mode, and most responses would fall within two standard deviations of the mode. Clearly, the distribution in Figure 7.1 is not normal. The mean lies above the mode, and significant responses exist three standard deviations above (but not below) the mean, giving the curve the characteristics of positive skew. Statistics exist for calculating skewness of a distribution, but the visual effect suffices in this case.

Why would creative thinking be positively skewed? More particularly, why would response to the TAT blank card be positively skewed? The answer to this second question may not automatically apply to creative

Table 7.2. Comparisons of Skew for Untimed Test Scores

Variable	Skewness	
	Presented Items	Invented Items
Patterns and Lines	1.13	1.49
Instances	0.48	1.65
Uses	0.16	1.98
Similarities	0.46	−0.16
TAT Card Responses		
College Female	1.17	1.81
College Male	0.27	0.52

Note: The coefficient of relative skewness was determined from studies for which original data were available. Original data for Instances, Uses, and Similarities, courtesy of Dr. M.A. Runco.

thinking in general, but comparisons with responses to other creative-thinking exercises can be made to explore the problem of generality.

Positive skew (as portrayed in Figures 6.1 and 7.1) can reflect a number of factors unrelated to creativity, but in measurement, positively skewed scores are commonly the result of a test that is difficult (Cronbach, 1984, p. 179). Tests with such a distribution might be used to distinguish among the best members of a group of applicants, to determine exemptions from some requirement, or to award scholarships. The piling of scores at the lower end of the distribution is known as a "floor effect," and can be contrasted with negative skew, or "ceiling effect."

Although blank card response lengths are not test scores, there is reason to believe that they can be treated as such. One need only recall Tomkins' (1947) characterization of the blank card as a "testing of limits" (p. 23), or Henry's (1956) statement that "the importance of this [card] lies in the extreme challenge which it makes for the subject who must create for himself the entire scene as well as its people, events and plot development" (p. 46). The blank card responses seem to be positively skewed by the extreme imaginative challenge of the task.

Is such a task atypical in creativity measurement? There is much in findings already presented to argue that response to the TAT blank card is not atypical of creative-thinking tasks, and that creative thinking is typically a response to a task of relative difficulty in comparison to corresponding problem-solving tasks. Table 7.2 presents calculations of the "coefficient of relative skewness," a measure of the degree of asymmetry in a distribution (Glass & Stanley, 1970, p. 89), for six matched pairs of measures. One of each pair called for the subject to find a problem before solving it expressively, and the other simply called for expressive (usually divergent) solutions to presented problems. In five of the six cases, the coefficient of relative skewness is higher for the invented items than for the presented items. Positive skew does seem to be generally associated with response to invented items in comparison to corresponding tasks which call only for solving problems.

Creative thinking is demanding, and this may explain why the challenge of thinking creatively is met well by relatively few. Those who seek this challenge appear to be motivated by it, becoming far more responsive than the norm (cf. Albert, 1988). There is some argument as well as evidence to support this conception of creative thinking as difficult, even under optimal conditions.

The strenuousness of creative thinking has been described by Maddi (1975) in an article that is highly critical of the "actualization" approach to creativity. In this article, Maddi argues that creative thinking is far more difficult than proponents of the situational model of developing creativity (who advocate environmental freedom) assume. The proponents of freedom in the classroom seem to emphasize "permissive, unstructured circumstances" but at the same time overlook the values of "persistence, authenticity, and self-reliance" (p. 175) necessary to creative production. The "exercise of imagination in the direction of producing something not only useful but new" is seen as inherently difficult and requiring extreme exertion.

There is much to be said for Maddi's view. The evidence presented here indicates that even under near optimal conditions for creative response to a test, sustained creative thinking for most if not all individuals is very difficult. "Most if not all" is a qualification introduced by a question of perception. What seems impossible to one individual may be quite possible and even enjoyable for another. That is one reason why the analogy to a difficult test is so apt. It gives one a way to characterize how freedom to find a problem and solve it might be perceived objectively, but the perceptions of individuals taking a test might be quite different. Individuals who score low might consider the task almost impossible. Individuals who score high may be aware of the difficulty, but the high scoring individuals may also enjoy the sense of mastery that they derive from the task.

Freedom to find a problem and solve it in one's own way may be the *sine qua non* of creative expression without suggesting creative expression is easy. It is, however, easier under "open" problem and solution conditions than under more constraining conditions, in which creative expression can be more difficult, if not impossible, even for the creatively gifted. In terms of the TAT, Roe (1946b) characterized the response of participating artists as "appalled." Asking them to tell stories in response to pictures did not provide them the opportunity to imagine a picture of their own, in response to which they might have been able to be more imaginative, if not creative. We do not know what the artists might have done with the blank card. We do know that the TAT pictures evoked little in the way of creative response.

If the significance of freedom is overlooked, and one assumes that creative individuals create their own opportunities, one needs to look again. The logical alternative to the constructive activity of the artist is destructiveness, sometimes of the self. The theme of artistic alienation and the tendency to self-destruction is present in American literature and art, from the literature of the Beat Generation to the principal theme of the 1989 film *Dead Poets' Society*. One also finds that the potential for alienation or self-destruction of creative individuals is an undercurrent in the comments of creativity researchers, from Roe's (1946b) experience with dismayed but successful artists, to Torrance's (1984) description of his earliest experiences with creative students—"I punished them and punished them, about the only thing I knew then to do" (p. 153).

Fortunately, as Torrance indicated, the talents of creative individuals often survive such experiences, but denying creative thinkers the opportunity to be challenged by some form of intellectual freedom, or denying them the support of a sympathetic audience, can lead to wasted talent. So too can a general attitude of permissiveness, as Maddi (1975) pointed out. Speaking some years ago about inventors, Edwin Land (1964), the former president of Polaroid, remarked that organized society faces a paradox. On the one hand, it must resist change to preserve stability and structure, but on the other hand must make cautious substitutions for old arrays of order if society is to remain healthy and survive. The solution for society lies in various ways to challenge and protect the creative individual during the period in which his or her thoughts are developing.

CREATIVE THINKING AND CONFORMITY

The subject of conformity, or behavior in accordance with prevailing modes or customs, has long been related to creativity research. Summing up presentations by Erik Fromm, J.P. Guilford, Ernest Hilgard, Abraham Maslow, Rollo May, Margaret Mead, Henry Murray, Carl Rogers, and others at an early symposium on creativity, H.H. Anderson (1959, p. 256) stated that "the most consistent protest in the book is against *conformity*." A few years later, Crutchfield (1962) wrote what was perhaps the best article on "Conformity and Creative Thinking," although a significant amount of research and speculation continued to be published over the next few years (Moustakas, 1967; Starkweather & Cowling, 1967; Torrance, 1965, pp. 187–204). Since the 1960s, however, the term *conformity* has almost dropped from the lexicon of creativity researchers. Two rare exceptions are MacKinnon's (1978) book, *In Search of Human Effectiveness* and Albert and Runco's (1986) chapter in Sternberg and Davidson's *Conceptions of Giftedness*.

Outside these two sources, why have creativity researchers lost interest in the subject of conformity? Has the topic been exhausted, or has it simply fallen out of fashion since the 1960s, or both? The best way to determine whether or not the subject was only a fad, or whether or not it was eventually exhausted, is to look at how the highly creative responses to the TAT blank card (as determined by the creativity index) treat the subject of conformity, if it is treated at all, and to look at this thematic content in light of what is known about conformity.

Two of the six responses with the highest creativity indices (Cases 1 and 24 in Appendix B) were given by fine arts students and were analyzed in Chapter 6. They are not among the three stories with the highest creativity indices and will not be analyzed here. The four other relatively lengthy responses are presented in Appendix C. They take only a few minutes to read, and what the reader will find may inform as well as occasionally delight—two hallmarks of art, even though none of the four responses was given by an arts student.

If the subject were only a fad, one would not expect what might be called highly creative responses to the TAT blank card to contain much about conformity. As a subject, it would not be on the minds of these midwestern students in the 1980s as opposed to, say, students in Berkeley in the early 1960s. What is found upon reading the blank card stories with the highest creativity indices is that most manifest the theme of conformity as the problem which motivates a plot.

The graduate chemistry student (Case 46) told a story about two men from different eras who encounter each other on a road. One is from the past and the other is from the present, and the story revolves around what each is thinking about the other. There is drama but no action. The central theme of this story is revealed by the puzzlement and questioning of both characters. The central question is, what is normal? The problem is revealed from the very beginning when different fashions of clothing conflict, and the conflict begins to motivate the plot around the question of normalcy.

The implicit answer to the question is that normalcy is relative, varying from individual to individual. Deviance from the mode is viewed with suspicion by others as well as oneself, so the resolution to the story—each individual going his own way—assumes a very relativistic answer to the question. What is normal is what is acceptable to you. This resolution of the central conflict is far removed from an endorsement of conforming behavior. Whether or not one should conform to the expectations of another was an important question for this respondent, and the rather clear answer was "no."

No one would suggest that the theme of conformity is central to the story told by the nursing student (Case 58), which is about the vacation of a beaver family, but the theme of conformity is not absent. Getzels and Jackson (1962) noted that creative children tell stories to TAT pictures that debunk "conventional forms and stereotyped ideals" (p. 105). The stereotypes that are drubbed in this story are the ideals of "father knows best" and "the relaxing vacation." Here father beaver makes an error when he leads the family to a vacation in the city. The vacation proves to be a terrifying but harmless experience. The geographic details assure the authenticity of this response, which is in the mode of a children's story.

Conformity is more central to the plots of the other two stories. The undecided general studies major (Case 63), who was the only male in this group, told a story about a socially displaced upper-middle-class individual. The story begins with a description of a "huge" tower which houses a civilization much like our own but which is not made up of the human race. Humans have become extinct ("because they couldn't handle themselves"). Lower-class members of this society live on lower floors, and upper-class members live on upper floors of this delapidated tower.

The accidental displacement of one of the upper-middle-class inhabitants ("on the 70th story or so of this place") to the lower, less affluent floors poses the problem: What does one do about a discovery that challenges the old array, or that challenges social conventions? The eventual attempt to change the beliefs of his own social stratum to benefit the poorer members of society turns out to be disastrous for the hero, who is thrown to his death. Again authenticity is validated by the details. In this case, the subject pointed out a small spot on the blank card where the hero's body landed.

The psychology major (Case 75) also told a story in which the refusal to conform plays a prominent part. In this long, rollicking romance, stereotypes (e.g., the white knight, the elderly king, and the eligible princess) are dismissed in favor of more human characters: a princess who is in love with the court jester; a jester who challenges the white knight to win the princess; a princess who rescues her love from the battle; and the pair of lovers, who are banished to "live in shame" until the old king dies. The return of the couple to rule the kingdom is more than a happily-ever-after ending. In contrast to the story told about the huge tower, this unconventional romance ends on a note of optimism. Nonconformity triumphs to form the new social order.

In each of these cases, personal familiarity with a story type (children's adventure story, science fiction, or romance) may have made easier the extremely difficult task of telling a long story in response to the blank card, but none of these four stories came from language or arts majors. They all contained good problems or conflicts that seemed to permit logical resolutions (plot developments). The conflicts, however, tended to be between individuals and conventional expectations. Far from being a minor topic, the subject of conformity appears to have been predominant in three out of four of these cases.

Although the turbulence of the 1960s has passed, and conformity may not always be a major social issue, the issue remains alive for individuals who responded creatively to the blank card of the TAT. Why might this be so? Some of the best research about conformity and creative thinking does no more than raise the question about the relationship of the creative thinker to modal or conventional thinking. Crutchfield ended his excellent article by quoting Camus' (1958, p. 33) acceptance speech for the Nobel Prize:

> the man who, as often happens, chose the path of art because he was aware of his difference soon learns that he can nourish his art, and his difference, solely by admitting his resemblance to all. The artist fashions himself in that ceaseless oscillation from himself to others, midway between the beauty he cannot do without and the community from which he cannot tear himself. This is why true artists scorn nothing. They force themselves to understand instead of judging.

This profound observation suggests that the importance of the community for the creative thinker lies in a dynamic relationship between the general similarity and specific difference which permits self-definition. If Camus was right, the creative individual is literally trying to tear him- or herself free from the "mode," driven to distinguish the self from the group, but at the same time, driven to understand what is similar to the group in him- or herself.

For that reason, questions need to be raised about educational practices for creative individuals. Both Camus and Land have spoken clearly from very different viewpoints about the relation of the creative individual to social norms. Both indicated that an appreciation of the norm is necessary for creative individuals to make their unique contribution. Pepinsky (1960) and Torrance (1965) suggested that effective and creative individuals develop special strategies for relating (and reacting) to the norm group successfully.

The end of the 1980s and the beginning of the 1990s saw the emergence of tension between arts communities and the wider society in several incidents revolving around display of controversial paintings, photographs, and other works of art. In one incident, the display of a painting at a private showing in an art school so outraged some of the local citizenry that it produced a volatile and potentially dangerous situation (M. Field, personal communication, June 6, 1988). Although many viewed the crisis as posing a conflict between First Amendment rights and forces favoring censorship, the Constitutional issue did not address the distrust generated by the incident between many members of the wider community and the art school.

Distrust temporarily brought the threat of external evaluation. We know from research (Amabile, 1983) that an atmosphere of external evaluation would have inhibited creativity, but the threat was successfully resisted. This resolution did not, however, address the more fundamental question for arts education: What is the optimal relationship between an artist and his or her society? Although conformity to group expectations is not desirable in all ways, it is certainly desirable in some, and to some extent may be necessary for the development of an individual's artistic talent. Intellectual, emotional, or social isolation of artists from the wider society may not only deprive society of its creative thinkers, but may also deprive creative thinkers of their potential contribution to society.

A fruitful relationship between an artist and his or her society cannot be compelled by law. As the board of trustees of the art school recognized, such a relationship can only be established through mutual trust, so that the artist may be protected in his or her freedom to create, and society in return may be given the artist's vision, which often reflects social modes or conventions from another perspective. In educating artistic talent, certainly some differential treatment of creative talent is desirable—but how much, and how early? What needs to be cultivated, among both the mode and the extreme with regard to creative talent, is mutual trust rather than judgments that reflect a potentially tragic alienation.

Far from exhausted, the topic of creative thinking and conformity will continue to demand attention whenever the majority seek to compel conformity to community standards of arts, or whenever artists seek to develop their thoughts, feelings, or social relationships in isolation from the wider community.

CREATIVE THINKING AND EDUCATION

The topic of creative thinking and education has typically been handled either through very general and largely speculative essays, or through evaluations of specific programs. Essays were common in the 1960s but were less common in the 1980s. With respect to creative thinking, critical essays tended to punish education for its solitary focus on convergent thinking, and more optimistic treatises assumed that anyone could become a creative thinker, regardless of his or her personality orientation. The positive effect of the general criticism was to sensitize educators to the need to understand the creative individual. Enthusiastic promotion of creative thinking likewise had a constructive effect, motivating educators to adopt some of the philosophical assumptions that led to altered methods and occasional curricular reform, particularly for students labeled as creatively gifted.

Perhaps as a part of the accountability movement in education as a whole in the 1980s, program evaluation became the common type of educational article about creative thinking. The interest in program evaluation may have reached a peak with the publication of Torrance's (1986) survey of the effectiveness of over 300 attempts to teach creative thinking skills. Among these were 36 creative arts programs used as vehicles to teach creative thinking, with an average success rate of 81 percent in 1972 and 73 percent in 1983.

It is still too early to view the accountability movement in any historical perspective, but in the 1980s, art educators were tending to challenge the assumption that creativity should be the principal goal of instruction in art. Criticism of 1960s approaches to art education joined a general "back to the basics" movement in education of the 1970s (Smith, 1979) to structure a program in art education in the 1980s known as Discipline Based Art Education, or DBAE.

Financially supported by the Getty Trust, this approach to art education based its curriculum on four principal components: creating art, art history, art criticism, and esthetics (Getty Center for Education in the Arts, 1985). In the article which laid the philosophical foundation for this approach (Clark, Day, & Greer, 1987), "the creative self-expression rationale" for art education, in which "art is seen as an instrument for developing what is assumed to be each child's inherent creativity and expressive abilities" (p. 133), was roundly criticized. Instead, the proponents of DBAE argued that art can be appreciated on a rational as well as an esthetic basis, and should be taught as a problem-solving process in its own right (Pariser, 1983).

The series of studies presented in this book suggest that although creative thinking for elementary age children can exist before the development of formal logic, perhaps by high school and certainly by college, creative thinking cannot proceed without it. Educationally, logical thinking often comes under the ruberic of "critical thinking," but whatever label deductive logic is given, it appears to be prerequisite to mature creative thinking. This line of reasoning leads one to reject the extreme view that every emphasis on convergent thinking, particularly in the elementary years, stifles creativity. An emphasis on the development of logical thinking actually lays the foundation for developments in creative thinking later on.

A unique emphasis on convergent thinking, however, fails to address the intuitive and expressive capabilities related to interest and achievement in the arts. Use of these skills and abilities begins when children are allowed to solve problems using their own methods. Within the DBAE model, Rush (1987) found that "tutored images" provide a method to guide children to increasing expressiveness as they solve some artistic problem presented by the teacher. This method of expressive problem solving appears to be effective with some children as young as kindergarten age. Similarly, in the language arts, Pfotenhauer (1982) found brainstorming to be an effective prewriting activity to help elementary students think of something to say about a topic. Resembling divergent thinking in some ways, brainstorming encourages expression through the generation of multiple possibilities, whether the possibilities are associative or logical in their origin.

It would be mistaken to assume, however, that all children are intuitive and expressive to the same degree. Furthermore, the extremes of these capabilities are combined with logic by relatively few in the difficult task of thinking creatively. In the extreme, intuitive perception calls for problem invention, and artistic expression calls for partial identification or empathy with individuals, situations, or even things (Margulies, 1989, pp. 14-18). Both intuition and empathy are difficult to combine with logic, and artists typically make the task easier for themselves by writing in a familiar genre or portraying a familiar topic. The need to provide instruction in creative thinking for artistically talented individuals in specific subjects seems no less urgent than the need to develop opportunities for expressive problem solving in general.

As a result, two levels of arts programs seem desirable, one for general appreciation and limited exploration of expression, and the other for individuals who are artistically talented. Such a division of programs is consistent with many of the existing curricula in art, language arts, music, and performing arts that utilize special ability groupings, particularly at the secondary level. What such a division of programs does not include, however, is general support for *creative* thinking throughout the academic curriculum.

There are two important implications here. First, because less than 20 percent of artistically oriented individuals can pursue (or choose to pursue) an artistic career, artistically oriented individuals should have opportunities to think creatively across the curriculum. These opportunities would allow creative thinkers to develop their talents through essays in which they designate their own topics, or through visual presentations of their own design. All courses of study should permit creative thinking to support the development of creative thinking among those who are capable of it in any subject—not just the arts. The development of logical thinking to some extent depends on its usefulness throughout the curriculum. We should expect that no less is required to permit the development of creative thinking.

A second advantage of mainstreaming creative thinking is that its general development allows for an appropriate social context for artistic individuals, whose talents can suffer from continual or careful segregation from less artistic individuals. To put the matter somewhat bluntly, creative individuals need to "feel normal" despite their differences from others. Perhaps they should receive special instruction in specialized classes, and exercise creative options in general classes. This need to feel normal and develop respect for their peers, as their peers develop respect for them, poses a problem for highly specialized instruction which may absorb the advanced student in a literary, musical, or visually artistic world. Although such experiences can refine skills and self-definition, such refinements may only be profitable after earlier, more conventional educational experiences.

• • •

The beginning of the 1990s was heralded with criticism of the lack of cultural knowledge and thinking skills of students at all levels, and with optimism regarding programs to teach higher-order thinking skills. Both the criticism and the optimism could be seen as extensions of earlier educational movements and emphases, forecasting renewed interest in creativity and creative thinking. Despite pressures to conduct more realistic research, some individuals continued to show interest in creativity as a topic of dissertations. Research on creative thinking was demonstrating itself to be a rather hardy perennial flower, surviving since Binet and Henri (1896) proposed techniques to measure the imagination. Interest in creative thinking appeared to be surviving on its own strength, not because of its proximity to a particular time or place or person. If research on creative thinking could be said to be utterly dependent on anything for its continued existence, it was interest in understanding human nature.

References

Adkins, D.C., & Kuder, G.F. (1940). The relation of primary mental abilities to activity preferences. *Psychometrika, 5,* 251-262.

Albert, R.S. (1988). How high should one climb to find common ground? *Creativity Research Journal, 1,* 52-59.

Albert, R.S., & Runco, M.A. (1986). The achievement of eminence: A model based on a longitudinal study of exceptionally gifted boys and their families. In R.J. Sternberg & J.E. Davidson (Eds.), *Conceptions of giftedness* (pp. 332-357). New York: Cambridge University Press.

Amabile, T.M. (1979). Effects of external evaluation on artistic creativity. *Journal of Personality and Social Psychology, 37,* 221-233.

Amabile, T.M. (1983). *The social psychology of creativity.* New York: Springer-Verlag.

Amabile, T.M. (1985). Motivation and creativity: Effects of motivational orientation on creative writers. *Journal of Personality and Social Psychology, 48,* 393-399.

Anderson, H.H. (1959). Creativity in perspective. In H.H. Anderson (Ed.), *Creativity and its cultivation* (pp. 236-267). New York: Harper & Row.

Arlin, P.K. (1975). Cognitive development in adulthood: A fifth stage? *Developmental Psychology, 11,* 602-606.

Arlin, P.K. (1977). Piagetian operations in problem finding. *Developmental Psychology, 13,* 297-298.

Astin, H.S. (1967). Career development during the high school years. *Journal of Counseling Psychology, 14,* 94-98.

Ausubel, D.P., Novak, J.D., & Hanesian, H. (1978). *Educational psychology: A cognitive view* (2nd ed.). New York: Holt, Rinehart and Winston.

Barron, F., & Harrington, D.M. (1981). Creativity, intelligence, and personality. *Annual Reviews of Psychology, 32,* 439-476.

Bellak, L. (1958). Creativity: Some random notes toward a systematic consideration. *Journal of Projective Techniques, 22,* 363-380.

Bellak, L. (1986). *The T.A.T., C.A.T., AND S.A.T. in clinical use* (4th ed.). New York: Grune & Stratton.

Binet, A., & Henri, V. (1896). La psychologie indivduelle. *Année Psychologique, 2,* 411-465.

Burchard, E.M.L. (1952). The use of projective techniques in the analysis of creativity. *Journal of Projective Techniques, 16,* 412–427.

Camus, A. (1958). Camus at Stockholm: The acceptance of the Nobel Prize. *Atlantic Monthly, 201,* 33–34.

Child, D., & Smithers, A. (1973). An attempted validation of the Joyce-Hudson scale of convergence and divergence. *British Journal of Educational Psychology, 43,* 57–62.

Clark, G.A., Day, M.D., & Greer, W.D. (1987). Discipline-based art education: Becoming students of art. *The Journal of Aesthetic Education, 21,* 129–193.

Clark, P.M., & Mirels, H.L. (1970). Fluency as a pervasive element in the measurement of creativity. *Journal of Educational Measurement, 7,* 83–86.

Cohen, J., & Cohen, P. (1975). *Applied multiple regression/correlation analysis for the behavioral sciences.* New York: Erlbaum.

Cooley, W.W. (1967). Interactions among interests, abilities, and career plans. *Journal of Applied Psychology Monographs, 51*(5, Pt. 2), 1–16.

Costa, P.T., & McCrae, R.R. (1985). *The NEO personality inventory manual.* Odessa, FL: Psychological Assessment Resources.

Cronbach, L.J. (1984). *Essentials of psychological testing* (4th ed.). New York: Harper & Row.

Cropley, A.J. (1967). Divergent thinking and science specialists. *Nature, 215,* 671–672.

Cropley, A.J., & Field, T.W. (1968). Intellectual style and high school science. *Nature, 217,* 1211–1212.

Crutchfield, R.S. (1962). Conformity and creative thinking. In H.E. Gruber, G. Terrell, & M. Wertheimer (Eds.), *Contemporary approaches to creative thinking* (pp. 120–140). New York: Atherton.

Csikszentmihalyi, M. (1988). Where is the evolving milieu? *Creativity Research Journal, 1,* 60–63.

Csikszentmihalyi, M., & Getzels, J.W. (1988). Creativity and problem finding in art. In F.H. Farley & R.W. Neperud (Eds.), *The foundations of aesthetics, art & art education* (pp. 91–116). New York: Praeger.

Davidson, J.E., & Sternberg, R.J. (1984). The role of insight in intellectual giftedness. *Gifted Child Quarterly, 28,* 58–64.

Davis, G.A., & Rimm, S. (1977). Identification and counseling of the creatively gifted. In N. Colangelo & R.T. Zaffrann (Eds.), *New voices in counseling the gifted* (pp. 225–236). Dubuque, IA: Kendall/Hunt.

Davis, G.A., & Rimm, S. (1982). GIFFI I and II: Instruments for identifying creative potential in the junior and senior high school. *Journal of Creative Behavior, 16,* 50–57.

Dillon, J.T. (1982). Problem finding and solving. *Journal of Creative Behavior, 16,* 97–111.

Einstein, A., & Infeld, L. (1938). *The evolution of physics.* New York: Simon & Schuster.

Ennis, R.H. (1989). Critical thinking and subject specificity. *Educational Researcher, 18,* 4–10.

Ennis, R.H., & Paulus, D.H. (1965). *Critical thinking readiness in grades 1–12* (Phase I, Deductive Reasoning in Adolescence, Cooperative Research Project No. OE 1680). Ithaca, NY: Cornell University.

Field, T.W., & Poole, M.E. (1970). Intellectual style and achievement of arts and science undergraduates. *British Journal of Educational Psychology, 40,* 338–341.
Firestein, R.L., & McCowan, R.J. (1988). Creative problem solving and communication behaviors in small groups. *Creativity Research Journal, 1,* 106–114.
Gardner, H. (1982). *Art, mind, and brain.* New York: Basic Books.
Gardner, M. (1978). *aha! Insight.* San Francisco, CA: Freeman.
Getty Center for Education in the Arts. (1986). *Beyond creating: The place for art in America's schools.* Los Angeles, CA: Author.
Getzels, J.W. (1975). Problem-finding and the inventiveness of solutions. *Journal of Creative Behavior, 9,* 12–18.
Getzels, J.W., & Csikszentmihalyi, M. (1967). Scientific creativity. *Science Journal, 3,* 80–84.
Getzels, J.W., & Csikszentmihalyi, M. (1976). *The creative vision: A longitudinal study of problem finding in art.* New York: Wiley & Sons.
Getzels, J.W., & Jackson, P. W. (1962). *Creativity and intelligence: Explorations with gifted students.* New York: John Wiley & Sons.
Glass, A.L., Holyoak, K.J., & Santa, J.L. (1979). *Cognition.* Reading, MA: Addison-Wesley.
Glass, G.V., & Stanley, J.C. (1970). *Statistical methods in education and psychology.* Englewood Cliffs, NJ: Prentice-Hall.
Goodman, N. (1976). *Languages of art* (2nd ed.). Indianapolis, IN: Hackett Publishing.
Gottfredson, G.D., & Holland, J.L. (1975). Vocational choices of men and women: A comparison of predictors from the self-directed search. *Journal of Counseling Psychology, 22,* 28–34.
Gottfredson, G.D., Holland, J.L., & Gottfredson, L.S. (1975). The relation of vocational aspirations and assessments to employment reality. *Journal of Vocational Behavior, 7,* 135–148.
Guilford, J.P. (1956). The structure of intellect. *Psychological Bulletin, 53,* 267–293.
Guilford, J.P. (1967). *The nature of human intelligence.* New York: McGraw-Hill.
Guilford, J.P. (1975). Creativity: A quarter century of progress. In I.A. Taylor & J.W. Getzels (Eds.), *Perspectives in creativity* (pp. 37–59). Chicago: Aldine.
Guilford, J.P., Wilson, R.C., Christensen, P.R., & Lewis, D.J. (1951). *A factor-analytic study of creative thinking. I. Hypotheses and descriptions of tests* (Reports from the Psychological Laboratory, No. 4). Los Angeles, CA: University of Southern California.
Haddon, F.A., & Lytton, H. (1971). Primary education and divergent-thinking abilities—Four years on. *British Journal of Educational Psychology, 41,* 136–147.
Hansen, J.C., & Stocco, J.L. (1980). Stability of vocational interests of adolescents and young adults. *Measurement and Evaluation in Guidance, 13,* 173–178.
Hargreaves, D.J., & Bolton, N. (1972). Selecting creativity tests for use in research. *British Journal of Psychology, 63,* 451–462.
Harrington, D.M. (1975). Effects of explicit instructions to "be creative" on the psychological meaning of divergent thinking test scores. *Journal of Personality, 43,* 434–454.
Hattie, J.A. (1977). Conditions for administering creativity tests. *Psychological Bulletin, 84,* 1249–1260.

Hattie, J.A. (1980). Should creativity tests be administered under testlike conditions? *Journal of Educational Psychology, 72,* 87–98.

Henry, W. (1956). *The analysis of fantasy: The thematic apperception test in the study of personality.* New York: Wiley.

Hocevar, D. (1979). *The development of the creative behavior inventory.* Paper presented at the meeting of the Rocky Mountain Psychological Association. (ERIC Document Reproduction Service No. ED 170 350)

Hocevar, D. (1980). Intelligence, divergent thinking, and creativity. *Intelligence, 4,* 25–40.

Holland, J.L. (1959). A theory of vocational choice. *Journal of Counseling Psychology, 6,* 35–45.

Holland, J.L. (1985a). *Making vocational choices* (2nd ed.). Englewood Cliffs, NJ: Prentice-Hall.

Holland, J.L. (1985b). *The self-directed search: Professional manual.* Odessa, FL: Psychological Assessment Resources.

Hudson, L. (1966). *Contrary imaginations.* London: Methuen.

Hudson, L. (1968). *Frames of mind.* London: Methuen.

Hudson, L. (1987). Creativity. In R.L. Gregory (Ed.), *The Oxford companion to the mind* (pp. 171–172). Oxford: Oxford University Press.

Inhelder, B., & Piaget, J. (1958). *The growth of logical thinking from childhood to adolescence.* New York: Basic Books.

Instructional Objectives Exchange. (1971). *Judgment: Deductive logic and assumption recognition.* Los Angeles, CA: Author.

Jausovec, N. (1989). Affect in analogical transfer. *Creativity Research Journal, 2,* 255–266.

Jordaan, J.P., & Heyde, M.B. (1979). *Vocational maturity during the high school years.* New York: Teachers College Press.

Kelso, G.I., Holland, J.L., & Gottfredson, G.D. (1977). The relation of self-reported competencies to aptitude test scores. *Journal of Vocational Behavior, 10,* 99–103.

Kirkland, J. (1974). Divergent thinking and academic course orientation. *Psychological Reports, 35,* 518.

Klatsky, R.L. (1980). *Human memory* (2nd ed.). San Francisco, CA: Freeman.

Lamb, R.R., & Prediger, D.J. (1981). *Technical report for the unisex edition of the ACT Interest Inventory (UNIACT).* Iowa City, IA: American College Testing Program.

Land, E.H. (1964). The role of invention in organized society. *Product Engineering, 34,* 60–62.

Lloyd-Bostock, S.M.A. (1979). Convergent-divergent thinking and arts-science orientation. *British Journal of Psychology, 70,* 155–163.

McCrae, R.R. (1987). Creativity, divergent thinking, and openness to experience. *Journal of Personality and Social Psychology, 52,* 1258–1265.

McHenry, R.E., & Shouksmith, G.A. (1970). Creativity, visual imagination and suggestibility. *British Journal of Educational Psychology, 40,* 154–160.

Mackay, C.K., & Cameron, M.B. (1968). Cognitive bias in Scottish first-year science and arts undergraduates. *British Journal of Educational Psychology, 38,* 315–318.

MacKinnon, D.W. (1960). The highly effective individual. *Teachers College Record, 61,* 367-378.
MacKinnon, D.W. (1978). *In search of human effectiveness.* Buffalo, NY: Creative Education Foundation.
Macworth, N.H. (1965). Originality. *American Psychologist, 20,* 51-66.
Maddi, S.R. (1975). The strenuousness of the creative life. In I.A. Taylor & J.W. Getzels (Eds.), *Perspectives in creativity* (pp. 173-190). Chicago: Aldine.
Magnusson, D., & Backteman, G. (1978). Longitudinal stability of person characteristics: Intelligence and creativity. *Applied Psychological Measurement, 2,* 481-490.
Margulies, A. (1989). *The empathic imagination.* New York: W.W. Norton.
Matarazzo, J.D. (1972). *Wechsler's measurement and appraisal of adult intelligence* (5th ed.). Baltimore, MD: Williams & Wilkins.
Mednick, S.A. (1976). The associative basis of the creative process. In A. Rothenberg & C.R. Hausman (Eds.), *The creativity question* (pp. 227-237). Durham, NC: Duke University.
Mednick, S.A., & Mednick, M.T. (1967). *Examiner's manual: Remote associates test.* Boston: Houghton Mifflin.
Meyer, R.E. (1983). *Thinking, problem solving, cognition.* San Francisco, CA: Freeman.
Milgram, R.M., & Milgram, N.A. (1976). Creative thinking and creative performance in Israeli students. *Journal of Educational Psychology, 68,* 255-259.
Moerdyk, A. (1971). Divergency and creativity. *Journal of Behavioral Science, 1,* 107-108.
Moore, H. (1985). Notes on sculpture. In B. Ghiselin (Ed.), *The creative process* (pp. 68-73). Berkeley, CA: University of California. (Originally published in 1952)
Moore, M.T. (1985). The relationship between the originality of essays and variables in the problem-discovery process. *Research in the Teaching of English, 19,* 84-95.
Moustakas, C. (1967). Creativity and conformity in education. In R.L. Mooney & T.A. Razik (Eds.), *Explorations in creativity* (pp. 173-184). New York: Harper & Row.
Murray, H.A. (1943). *The thematic apperception test and manual.* Cambridge, MA: Harvard.
Nabokov, V. (1981). *Lectures on Russian literature* (F. Bowers, Ed.). New York: Harcourt Brace Jovanovich.
Nagy, P., & Griffiths, A.K. (1982). Limitations of recent research relating Piaget's theory to adolescent thought. *Review of Educational Research, 52,* 513-556.
Noble, C.E. (1952). An analysis of meaning. *Psychological Review, 59,* 421-430.
Nuttall, D.L. (1973). Convergent and divergent thinking. In H.J. Butcher & H.B. Pont (Eds.), *Educational research in Great Britain 3* (pp. 112-129). London: University of London.
O'Keefe, G. (1976). *Georgia O'Keefe.* New York: Viking.
Osipow, S.H. (1973). *Theories of career development* (2nd ed.). Englewood Cliffs, NJ: Prentice-Hall.
Pariser, D. (1983). The arts, cognition, and craft: Implications for teaching and

research. *Art Education, 36,* 50–57.
Pepinsky, P.N. (1960). A study of productive nonconformity. *Gifted Child Quarterly, 4,* 81–85.
Pfotenhauer, V. (1982). Brainstorming as a prewriting activity. *Childhood Education, 59,* 111–113.
Povey, R.M. (1970). Arts/science differences: Their relationship to curriculum specialization. *British Journal of Psychology, 61,* 55–64.
Prediger, D.J. (1982). Dimensions underlying Holland's hexagon: Missing link between interests and occupations? *Journal of Vocational Behavior, 21,* 259–287.
Reitman, W.R. (1964). Heuristic decision procedures, open constraints, and the structure of ill-defined problems. In M.W. Shelly & G.L. Bryan (Eds.), *Human judgments and optimality* (pp. 282–315). New York: Wiley & Sons.
Reitman, W.R. (1965). *Cognition and thought: An information-processing approach.* New York: Wiley & Sons.
Rimm, S. (1980). *Group inventory for finding creative talent.* Watertown, WI: Educational Assessment Service, Inc.
Rimm, S., & Davis, G.A. (1980). Five years of international research with GIFT: An instrument for the identification of creativity. *Journal of Creative Behavior, 14,* 35–46.
Roberge, J.J., & Paulus, D.H. (1971). Developmental patterns for children's class and conditional reasoning abilities. *Developmental Psychology, 4,* 191–200.
Roe, A. (1946a). Painting and personality. *Rorschach Research Exchange, 10,* 86–100.
Roe, A. (1946b). The personality of artists. *Educational and Psychological Measurement, 6,* 401–408.
Roe, A. (1953). A psychological study of eminent psychologists and anthropologists, and a comparison with biological and physical scientists. *Psychological Monographs, 67* (Whole No. 352).
Rosenzweig, S., & Fleming, E.E. (1949). Apperceptive norms for the Thematic Apperception Test. *Journal of Personality, 17,* 475–503.
Rump, E.E. (1982). Relationships between creativity, arts-orientation, and esthetic-preference variables. *Journal of Psychology, 110,* 11–20.
Rump, E.E., & Dunn, M. (1971). Extensions to the study of science students' divergent thinking ability. *Nature, 229,* 349–350.
Runco, M.A. (1986). Divergent thinking and creative performance in gifted and nongifted children. *Educational and Psychological Measurement, 46,* 375–384.
Runco, M.A. (1989). The creativity of children's art. *Child Study Journal, 19,* 177–189.
Runco, M.A., & Albert, R.S. (1985). The reliability and validity of ideational originality in the divergent thinking of academically gifted and nongifted children. *Educational and Psychological Measurement, 45,* 483–501.
Runco, M.A., & Okuda, S.M. (1988). Problem discovery, divergent thinking, and the creative process. *Journal of Youth and Adolescence, 17,* 213–222.
Rush, J.C. (1987). Interlocking images: The conceptual core of a discipline-based art lesson. *Studies in Art Education, 28,* 206–220.
Schmidt, R.A. (1988). *Motor control and learning* (2nd ed.). Champaign, IL: Human Kinetics.
Schwabel, M. (1975). Formal operations in first-year college students. *Journal of Psychology, 91,* 133–141.

Scott, L.E. (1988). A comparative study of personality, values, and background characteristics of artistically talented, academically talented, and average 11th and 12th grade students. *Studies in Art Education, 29*, 292–301.

Simpson, E.J. (1972). *The classification of educational objectives: Psychomotor domain.* Urbana, IL: University of Illinois.

Singer, D.L., & Whiton, M.B. (1971). Ideational creativity and expressive aspects of human figure drawing in kindergarten-age children. *Developmental Psychology, 4*, 366–369.

Smilansky, J. (1984). Problem solving and the quality of invention. *Journal of Educational Psychology, 76*, 377–386.

Smilansky, J., & Halberstadt, N. (1986). Inventors versus problem solvers. *Journal of Creative Behavior, 20*, 183–201.

Smith, R.T. (1979). Concepts, concept learning, and art education. *Review of Research in Visual Arts Education, 11*, 7–15.

Smithers, A.G., & Child, D. (1974). Convergers and divergers: Different forms of neuroticism? *British Journal of Educational Psychology, 44*, 304–306.

Snow, C.P. (1963). *The two cultures* (2nd ed.). Cambridge, England: Cambridge University Press.

Souriau, P. (1881). *Théorie de l'invention.* Paris: Librairie Hachette.

Starkweather, E.K., & Cowling, F.G. (1967). The measurement of conforming and nonconforming behavior in preschool children. In R.L. Mooney & T.A. Razik (Eds.), *Explorations in creativity* (pp. 229–238). New York: Harper & Row.

Sternberg, R.J. (1986). *Intelligence applied.* New York: Harcourt Brace Jovanovich.

Sternberg, R.J., & Davidson, J.E. (1983). Insight in the gifted. *Educational Psychologist, 18*, 51–57.

Sternberg, R.J., & Kastoor, B. (1986). Synthesis of research on the effectiveness of intellectual skills programs. *Educational Leadership, 44*, 60–67.

Strong, E.K. (1943). *Vocational interests of men and women.* Stanford, CA: Stanford University Press.

Subotnik, R.F. (1988). Factors from the structure of intellect model associated with gifted adolescents' problem finding in science. *Journal of Creative Behavior, 22*, 42–54.

Super, D.E. (1963). Vocational development in adolescence and early childhood: Tasks and behaviors, In D.E. Super, R. Starischevsky, N. Matlin, & J.P. Jordaan (Eds.), *Career development: Self concept theory* (Research monograph No. 4). New York: College Entrance Examination Board.

Super, D.E. (1969). The natural history of a study of lives and vocations. *Perspectives on Education, 2*, 13–22.

Super, D.E., & Overstreet, P.L. (1960). *The vocational maturity of ninth-grade boys.* New York: Columbia University.

Thurstone, L.L. (1938). *Manual of instructions for tests for primary mental abilities.* Washington, DC: American Council on Education.

Tomkins, S.S. (1947). *The Thematic Appercention Test: The theory and technique of interpretation.* New York: Grune & Stratton.

Torrance, E.P. (1965). *Rewarding creative behavior.* Englewood Cliffs, NJ: Prentice-Hall.

Torrance, E.P. (1967). The Minnesota studies of creative behavior: National and

international extensions. *Journal of Creative Behavior, 1,* 137-154.
Torrance, E.P. (1974a). *Torrance tests of creative thinking.* Bensenville, IL: Scholastic Testing Service.
Torrance, E.P. (1974b). *Torrance tests of creative thinking: Directions manual and scoring guide for verbal test booklet b.* Lexington, MA: Personnel Press.
Torrance, E.P. (1984). The role of creativity in identification of the gifted and talented. *Gifted Child Quarterly, 28,* 153-156.
Torrance, E.P. (1986). Teaching creative and gifted learners. In M.C. Wittrock (Ed.), *Handbook of research on teaching* (3rd ed., pp. 630-647). New York: Macmillan.
Tyler, L.E. (1964). The antecedents of two varieties of vocational interests. *Genetic Psychology Monographs, 70,* 177-227.
Vondracek, F.W., & Lerner, R.M. (1982). Vocational role development in adolescence. In B.B. Wolman (Ed.), *Handbook of developmental psychology* (pp. 602-614). Englewood Cliffs, NJ: Prentice-Hall.
Wakefield, J.F. (1985). Towards creativity: Problem finding in a divergent thinking exercise. *Child Study Journal, 15,* 265-270.
Wakefield, J.F. (1986). Creativity and the TAT blank card. *Journal of Creative Behavior, 20,* 127-133.
Wakefield, J.F. (1988). Problem finding in the arts and sciences. *Questioning Exchange, 2,* 133-140.
Wakefield, J.F. (1989). Creativity and cognition: Some implications for arts education. *Creativity Research Journal, 2,* 51-63.
Wallach, M.A. (1985). Creativity testing and giftedness. In F.D. Horowitz & M. O'Brien (Eds.), *The gifted and talented: Developmental perspectives* (pp. 99-124). Washington, DC: American Psychological Association.
Wallach, M.A., & Kogan, N. (1965). *Modes of thinking in young children.* New York: Holt, Rinehart and Winston.
Wertheimer, M. (1982). *Productive thinking.* Chicago, IL: University of Chicago. (Originally published in 1945)
Yčas, M.A., & Pascal, C.E. (1974). Convergent, divergent, and esthetic ability and bias in college students. *Improving Human Performance, 3,* 22-37.

appendix A
Occupations of Artistically Oriented Individuals

One of the persistent empirical difficulties in vocational interest assessment has been that although individual types can be identified (with the personality scale on which they score highest), and this identification seems adequately stable to make vocational predictions, individuals do not always choose their predicted vocations. For example, Table A.1 (derived from data tabulated by Gottfredson & Holland, 1975) shows percentages of men and women entering college with an arts orientation who express a choice of an artistic career either one or three years later. Although many artistically oriented students do choose artistic careers after three years, a larger percentage choose theoretically related vocations (i.e., social and investigative careers). Most of these individuals do choose one or the other adjacent vocational area (added evidence of the validity of the theory), but the percentage choosing nonartistic careers is still curiously high.

This situation is not complemented by investigative and social types choosing artistic careers, as one might expect if measurement error were responsible for the changes. Data from the source table reveal that although 11 percent of artistically oriented students expressed choice of scientific careers after three years, only 7 percent of scientifically oriented students expressed choice of artistic careers. Similarly, 36 percent of artistically oriented students chose social careers (such as counseling or teaching), but only 9 percent of socially oriented students chose artistic careers. The direction of change is not a statistical artifact: A larger percentage of artistically oriented individuals choose nonartistic careers than nonartistically oriented individuals choose artistic careers.

Lack of employment opportunity may be the reason why less than 2 percent of Americans become employed in artistic careers, while over

Table A.1. Artistically Oriented Individuals Choosing Artistic Careers*

College Sample	N	Percent Career Choice**					
		I	A	S	E	C	R
After 1 Year							
Men	28	14	<u>57</u>	25	0	4	0
Women	76	13	<u>39</u>	43	1	3	0
After 3 Years							
Men	49	12	<u>35</u>	24	22	2	4
Women	97	11	<u>28</u>	49	10	1	0

*Adapted from data in Gottfredson & Holland, 1975.
**In Holland's (1985a) typology, I is Investigative, A is Artistic, S is Social, E is Enterprising, C is Conventional, and R is Realistic. Underlined percentages are predicted choices.

Table A.2. Percentages of Jobs and People*

Type of Work	Percent People	Percent Jobs	Ratio (P/J)
Investigative	15.3	7.4	2.1
Artistic	10.5	1.6	6.6
Social	43.4	15.6	2.8
Enterprising	3.7	18.7	0.2
Conventional	2.5	24.5	0.1
Realistic	20.4	34.3	0.6

*Adapted from data in Gottfredson, Holland, & Gottfredson, 1975. Reprinted by permission.

8 percent of men and almost 13 percent of women can be classified as artistic through their scores on the *Self-Directed Search* (Holland, 1985b, p. 77). The disparity between the employability of artistic and nonartistic types is evident in Table A.2 (derived from data tabulated by Gottfredson, Holland, & Gottfredson, 1975). Analysis reveals that percentages of people (according to predominant interest) and jobs (according to Holland's types) present much better odds for employment in nonartistic than in artistic areas, where the number of individuals employed (and perhaps, employable) is less than one-sixth of individuals who are artistically oriented.

The implication for personality orientations is that many individuals who might initially identify themselves as artistic do not become professional artists, but often choose scientific and social careers (which are also competitive). The extent to which these individuals express artistic talents through their work, make creative contributions in their fields, pursue creative hobbies, or are frustrated in the expression of their talents or misjudge them is unknown, but this topic deserves further research. Anecdotes about the artistic interests of creative scientists abound, and both scientific and social service occupations permit limited expression of esthetic values.

appendix B
Blank Card Stories by Fine Arts Majors

Modified instructions for the blank card: "See what you can see on this blank card. Imagine some picture there and describe it to me in detail, then tell me a story about it." Some repetitions and interjections in the responses were omitted to facilitate narrative flow.

Case 1
Sex: female
Age: 18 years 8 months
Major: music education
Creativity Index: 1.98
Blank Card Response:

Okay, I see a town with this, with a, some kind of a medieval place, and there's this big, fire-breathing dragon.

He lives just outside of town. You can see him out there because he's, he's just kind of over the hill, just sits there and smolders and looks at everything that's going on. And inside the town there's like a joker, and the—or the court jester—and all these musicians all running around having a great time.

And let's see. The dragon, he really isn't as bad as he likes to make everyone feel, but he just keeps everyone on their toes. And let's see what else. Oh, there's little kids running around in the street, and they have their dogs and cats and their little rabbits. And what else. It's like, it's like the town, like the middle of a, like the town square, so there's just all kinds of everything going on.

Let's see, there's people out in the streets, you know, yelling and selling stuff, and on top of the kids and the music. And let's see. Oh, there's the pub over there, so those guys in there are getting real rowdy, and the groups of women all running around. And you have people in their long gowns and hair and tall, pointy hats, and the men are all trudging around in boots and things. There's just a lot of noise and color everywhere. And out, on the out, and everything outside of the town—since it's not really all that big—there's lots of land, there's lots of trees and all kinds of plants and flowers, so, you know, there's lots of color and texture. And the buildings are all rough stones, and all different kinds of things.

And let's see. Oh, there's an ocean over here, because they have to have ships coming in to get to them. So they have real fancy tall ships with all the rigging and everything. And so there's people yelling, and the harbour's loading and unloading going on.

And what else. Oh well, I think that's pretty good. It's just, it's this town is like, it's showing more what's going on at that time more than just, like usually, story things that have just castles and stuff. But that's not part of it. These people are all having their own great life outside of everything the rich people own.

Case 24
Sex: female
Age: 20 years 3 months
Year in School: junior
Major: art education
Creativity Index: 1.89
Blank Card Response:

There is a little girl who had a pet dog, and she loved the dog a lot, but her mother did not know she had this dog. She didn't know that she was feeding this dog with her food from the table, so she has to keep the dog in hiding. And she keeps it in her basement. And she lets it out every night. And sometimes she keeps it in her club house when it wants to be fed. She sneaks the hose from the back of the house to give it a bath when her mother is gone, and she sneaks food from the cabinet to feed the dog while her mother is gone.

One day, her mother came home early from work, and she saw her out back playing with this big dog. As the mother approaches the young girl and the dog, the dog jumps up and bites the mother on the arm and takes off running. The little girl's frightened. She's frightened because the dog bit her mother, and that her mother is now hurt, but since the dog didn't bite her too awfully hard—she's okay—her mother asked her where the dog came from, and she said it was just one of the neighborhood dogs. And she asked if that was the same dog that's been, that she has been keeping in the basement and sneaking the food for. And she doesn't know what to say.

Her mother again asks her if that's the same dog. She finally says, "Yes, that's the same dog." Her mother asks her why she didn't tell her about the dog. She said that she thought she would make him go away or put him in the dog pound. Her mother explains to her that as long as she told her the truth, that she wouldn't have done, that she would have let her keep the dog if she wanted it bad enough.

Now the girl is sorry that she kept it in hiding for so long, because now it is gone, and she wished she hadn't of done that because now she would have had a dog, and they would've been happier. And maybe the dog wouldn't have bit her mother at all, because maybe the dog felt afraid of the mother, so she had never seen the, he's never seen the mother before.

So the mother goes to a dog pound and brings home a little puppy for the little girl. But first, before she'll give her the puppy, she tells the little girl to always tell her the truth and that things will come out better. So now the little girl and the mother are happy.

Case 33
Sex: male
Age: 20 years 6 months
Year in School: senior
Major: music education
Creativity Index: 1.47
Blank Card Response:

The sun beat down, and the hot wind occasionally blew this man stumbling through the desert. He wondered how he managed to lose his horse and his provisions. He was sure he was starting to delude, but for some reason he saw his entire life like the desert.

He saw that all along, there never really had been anything except what just seemed like flat sand. It seemed like there was never a river of meaning running through his life to which he could always return for refreshment. As he looked at the plants around him—the sagebrush and other desert plants—he just, he focused on the things that had always been there, the feelings that had always been there in his life regardless of the barrenness.

It made him wonder what would plants like that grow like if they were given as much water as they would have in a more moderate climate. Had those abilities and those dreams in his life always been there and just been unable to grow because he was never able to feed them enough water to allow them growth? Or were they, too, empty—dried up and blowing away like the tumbleweeds which occasionally crossed his path?

Mountains in the distance, there always seemed to be mountains in his life too. There always seemed to be some unavoidable and unscalable conflict to run into. There was no way around them. In actuality, they provided the only change of pace. Otherwise, it was just flat desert. Coming to a mountain was a challenge, certainly an exhausting one, but the sense of accomplishment...suddenly, he wished that he had been walking in a much more mountainous region.

Case 50
Sex: female
Age: 21 years 5 months
Year in School: junior
Major: music education
Creativity Index: 1.80
Blank Card Response:

I see a colorful farm area, with a lot of hills, rolling hills and pastures. It's just like a patchwork. There are cattle over here, and there is a farm over here, a farm building, and the next hill has a barn on it. There is a sunset in the background, with trees all over, and there—it's not in modern day. It's more like in the pioneer days, and there are no fences, even though there is like a patchwork. There are plowed fields. There is one, there is a town where the townspeople are with their horses, and this is on a far hill. There are horses, just like in western days, and there are ladies in long beautiful gowns, very colorful. And then again, there are ladies in dull skirts that, that are the farm wives, whereas the city store owners have the beautiful dresses on. And the color is, the greenery of the grass is very bright, and yet the buildings and the, and the clothes of...are rather dull. Also the dresses of the wealthy women are colorful.

And there's a horse being drawn by a carriage, or drawing a carriage, and inside are, is a lady and a man and their child. And they are just passing through, going to another town, going away to spend Easter with their parents.

And they've come from Philadelphia and they're going to Illinois. It's not just for Easter, but it's, they haven't seen their parents, or their parents haven't seen their new child. They are going to take it to see their new child.

And as they're driving along the child, they stop and take a nap. And while they're stopping at this campground, they, the child, the parents are asleep, and the child wakes up and becomes animated, and goes and looks around in the woods, and sees all the animals and plays with them and talks to them. This child is just an infant, but yet he can, he can talk to the animals, and animals talk back to him, and they play. It's as if there's no time at all because the parents are still asleep, and yet the child has been playing in the woods for the last three days.

He finally eventually goes back to the parents after his little exploration trip, and all the while the child has to act again like a child, and like a baby, and can't speak, but yet in his mind, his mind is very advanced, and he just has all these experiences that his parents haven't realized or experienced or known he has experienced. And they, he grows up just like any other normal child, because children that pass through these woods, that, that happened to them. They, always the parents or families always fall asleep, and children always get up and do what they want to do. This child wanted to go out and play in the woods. Other children do whatever they want in that time.

Case 53
Sex: female
Age: 20 years 6 months
Year in School: junior
Major: art education
Creativity Index: .57
Blank Card Response:

I see a green cat sitting on a pillow. He's purring contentedly, sitting in a window he's looking out. And this cat right before, he was in this house, was before that, he was a sort of a stray. Nobody would have him because he was green.

Someone was, finally felt sorry for him and took him in. And he's just sitting in this window, sort of reflecting on one of his many lives. He's on, he's on his fifth life, and he's always been a normal cat until now. And he's sort of born a freak cat. And he's green—sort of a long-haired green cat. And this one, this woman found him starving in the alley and took him in and fed him until he was better.

And now he's found a home.

Case 70
Sex: female
Age: 19 years 11 months
Year in School: sophomore
Major: music education
Creativity Index: .62
Blank Card Response:

It's perhaps like maybe the Greek myths or something where there's a character that's carried up by Zeus or something and riding through the clouds. And the white blank is what that person kind of sees at the moment...it seems to be kind of labors, or whatever you want to call it....

appendix C
Blank Card Stories with High Creativity Indices

Case 46
Sex: female
Age: 23 years 11 months
College/Major: graduate/chemistry
Creativity Index: 2.24
Blank Card Response:

    I see two men standing there. One of them is standing beside a horse. He's wearing buckskins, has a musket, just has it over his shoulder, looking really sort of puzzled. The other man is dressed blue jeans, tee-shirt, standing beside a motorcycle. They're both out in the middle of the open prairie, and it's just sort of a dirt road.
    The man who's in buckskins has no idea what this thing is that's beside the other man. Never seen one before in his life. He's been up in the mountains for many, many years asleep. He started asking the man beside the motorcycle some questions, and the man beside the motorcycle is looking at him a little puzzled too because he doesn't know if the guy in the buckskins is just trying to con him, whether he is cracked in the head, or whether he's really found someone who's been asleep for over 100 years, because the man in the buckskin has told him some fantastic stories about what has happened in past history and things like this. You wouldn't really know much about it unless you had been there and lived it. At least this is what the guy beside the motorcycle is thinking.
    And the guy on the horse thinks this guy with the motorcycle is probably some friend of the devil because such a machine couldn't possibly

exist. And neither one knows what to make of the other one, and they don't really know what to do—whether they should just go their own ways or whether they should, you know, the guy on the horse doesn't know whether he should follow this guy on the motorcycle, or just go back where he came from. Because if he's that different, maybe a lot of other things are too, and he doesn't really want to change.

> *Case 58*
> *Sex:* female
> *Age:* 26 years 4 months
> *College/Major:* nursing
> *Creativity Index:* 2.08
> *Blank Card Response:*

Okay, I see a creek bed with overhanging trees. It's spring time and the sun is, the sun is filtering down through the trees, and it's creating different splashes of light and darkness on the ground, which is, which looks wet. There's tall grass along the creek bed, and there are rocks, rocks in the creek bed, and some logs which have fallen in. There are birds in the trees. The colors, the colors are basically dark green to a leafy-type of green, and yellow and dark brown.

And there are animals in the creek. Surprisingly enough, there are some beavers in the creek. The creek widens at a certain point, and there's a dam with sticks and mud. And this is the home of the beavers, and they have their holes along the creek bed also. And there's a family of beavers, male, female—mother, father—and two baby beavers. And oddly enough, the beavers can talk, and they can talk to each other by using spoken language, which happens to be English. And they can also communicate by slapping their tails around so that they have a signal system with their tails.

And the beavers are preparing to go on a vacation, a journey, and they are trying to decide how they can get from this creek to a river that they've heard about called the Illinois River and the town of Peoria. This is quite a ways from the town of Peoria, but these beavers are plotting among themselves, and they have their heads together and are talking very fast, and they're very hard to understand for anyone who would be trying to listen. Their tails are slapping around, and they're all, they're real excited. They're very enthusiastic about their trip. And they're deciding that they're reluctant to leave their dam because they're not at all sure what Peoria will be like. And they're thinking of perhaps locating underneath the bridge of I-74 which crosses the Illinois River at Peoria. This is their dream, and they're wondering how they're gonna, whether this is the right thing to do. But father beaver is very ambitious, and he says they must leave their town and their home hut, and they must travel to the big city.

So they set off. Father beaver's in the lead, with mother carrying baby beavers on her back, and they just start swimming down this creek until they get to a larger creek, the Mendota Creek, and from there they keep going until they get to this canal, and the canal takes them to a tributary of the Illinois River. And they keep swimming until they get to Peoria. And they're just, they're overwhelmed by the factory and the smoke and the sounds. And they cling to the side of the bridge, the side of the cliff underneath the bridge. And mother's terrified and father's terrified. Baby beavers are scared to death, and they're gnashing their teeth.

And the father says that this isn't at all what he thought it was gonna be, that other travelers had told a story of just this marvelous town, but if the, it was just, it was too much: The noise and the traffic and the bridge rumbled, and they decided that somehow they'd have to get back home. They just couldn't live like this, so they immediately turned around, dove down into the river, and their tails slapped against this river, and they took off swimming. And after an exhausted two weeks, they arrived back at their hut and decided that perhaps this was the best place to raise their children after all.

>Case 63
>Sex: male
>Age: 20 years 2 months
>College/Major: LAS/general curriculum (undecided)
>Creativity Index: 1.97
>Blank Card Response:

There's a huge, huge building on this piece of paper, and it's just a huge tower, and it's in the middle of nowhere. There's like, it's desolate desert all around this place. And this is like a 150-story-tall building, and it's just massive, it's huge. And what it is, is a place that there is a whole civilization living within this one tower because life is—as we know it—is no longer feasible.

These are not human beings. They have found that the human race has already been extinct because they couldn't handle themselves, so this civilization has set up a civilization within this huge, huge structure. All their society is arranged from top to bottom in this huge building, and it's just perfect because all of the low, poor people are on the bottom and all of the upperclass people are on the top of this building. And right now the building is not looking so good. There's a few, it, there's all tons of windows—it's like a Sears Tower or something—there's a few of them broken out and stuff.

And what has happened is, and these people have lived here in this civilization for a long, long time with no problem and peace. And everything is all, everything is made, they're all in social structures from lowest to top, but everybody's got their, their food, everybody lives. And all of this time everybody in each society has assumed that that was their place in society, so they accepted it.

But what happened was that one of these people, one of the upper-class people—he wasn't on the very top but he was in the upper middle class, he was about on the 70th story or so of this place—and what happened to this guy is, he accidentally got taken down to the lower class people, and he was exposed to what the other people see. Everybody lived in their separate, they, everybody knew everybody else was there, but they never saw each other. They never came in contact because they figured that would just cause problems.

But this guy inadvertently got tossed down and was exposed to a different way of life, and he got back, and he couldn't believe that there was a society structure like that because there was enough provisions and everything in this, within this whole building that everybody could live equally from the 1st floor all the way up to the 150th floor. And he was just totally amazed, and he couldn't understand why there was the lowest class because it's not like they had to be the low class. They could be the same as everybody else. It's just that whoever first started this thing set it up that way, and they don't know why.

But, so this guy started talking to some people about it, you know, he started talking to some of the wise people and stuff, and they couldn't handle this guy because, you know, he was telling them about this, and they says, "Well, that's...well, it may all be true and everything, but it cannot be done because that's the way it has always been."

And there's a little spot down on the bottom of this [points], around the bottom of this building, and what they have done is, the guys up there have all gotten together, and they chucked this guy out the window from the 70th floor, and he's just, he's dead down at the bottom. And nobody, and now it's, they're continuing on just like it was before.

(I bet you get unbelievable stories—all different kinds of stories from all these.)

Case 75
Sex: female
Age: 21 years 4 months
College/Major: LAS/psychology
Creativity Index: 2.65
Blank Card Response:

Okay, on this card is a big arena. Okay, and in this arena there are like, okay, on one side there's the king and the queen and his court and everything, and the court jester. And then the whole arena is just packed. And what they're going to watch is the knights. And the knights are going to hold a, you know, battle. It's one of those medieval times.

And so, we have the two knights—one knight all in white and one knight all in black. And what they want, what they have to do is, they have to, it's to the death. Okay, one of them is going to have to die, and the winner is going to win—what could he win?—the winner is going to win the kingdom from the king. Alright, the king is so involved in this that he has given up his throne or that, well, he's a very, he's a very sickly man, and he wants, he doesn't have a son. All he has is a daughter, okay, all he has is a daughter, and he knows that he is older and that he has to, and he doesn't have anybody to take over his reign, so whoever wins this will get to marry his daughter.

And so, alright, so the day comes, and the stadium is packed, and his daughter is in love with another man—neither of these knights. So then they hold the battle, and it lasts for a real long time, and one knight gets the advantage, and then the next knight gets the advantage. And it doesn't matter who wins—this girl is going to be very unhappy on either side. She's in love with the court jester.

Okay, so what happens is, alright, one knight finally loses, and so the maiden is like, "But I don't...." She told her dad that she didn't want to marry one of the knights, but he was nobility, and so "You have to do as I say...." And so when the knight in white wins, of course, so they, so he comes, and he takes off his mask and he says "My wife," or something like that, and so she just starts crying. She doesn't want to marry him.

So what the court jester does is he gets, he jumps out in the arena and he says, "I'm going to fight for my lady," and she says, "No, but you can't—it's not worth it" and blah, blah, blah. And he says, "But of course I will fight for you—if I have to lay down my life." So then what happens is he doesn't have a suit of armour or nothing, and so he has to fight anyway. So he goes and gets another horse—and he gets the knight in black's horse—and he uses that. And so he has to fight the knight in white.

Okay, so the battle begins, and the king is totally appalled. He says, "This is not the way I want my kingdom run," but the man just goes on. And all the people in the arena just think that it's great. And so what happens is, let's see, the girl goes over and lets out the lions' cage so the lions come out and all the bulls and everything like that. And so there's total chaos in the arena and everybody's cheering. They think it's really great, but the girl is so terribly distraught, she's so worried that she's going to lose her love.

So he finally manages to get out of the arena, leaving the knight in white there all by himself. And the lions get the knight in white. Well, the king must disown his daughter because she has totally appalled him. And now he doesn't know what to do because now he doesn't even have a daughter to get married off. So what he does is—let's see, what's he going to do?—I guess this is dragging out—he holds a contest between the knight, the court jester—well, what he does is he sends out his troops to get his daughter and the court jester. And they get him and they bring him back, and this father banishes them from the kingdom. He says, "You may never come back." And so the two go off, and they must live in shame, and they must hide from oh, all sorts of things.

But anyway, the king dies, and there's nobody to take over his kingdom. So the people are really worried there's nobody to take care of the kingdom, so the people hold a challenge for anybody who wants to come along. So what happens is all these people enter, and they have like the same sort of, well this one is, is who can kill the most lions. So there's this one outstanding person in the field who kills so many lions and everything like that, that they're going "Oh, he must be the king! He must be the king!"

And so it ends when he takes off his mask, and it's the jester, and well, he had to kill lions before when he had to fight the knight in white. So everybody's all happy because they really wanted the daughter to be the queen and the jester to be the king anyway.

Author Index

A
Adkins, D.C., 6, *95*
Albert, R.S., 40, 85, 86, *95*, *100*
Amabile, T.M., 23, 34, 35, 78, 90, *95*
Anderson, H.H., 86, *95*
Arlin, P.K., 14, 46, *95*
Astin, H.S., 49, *95*
Ausubel, D.P., 32, *95*

B
Backteman, G., 10, *99*
Barron, F., 6, 34, *95*
Bellak, L., 63, 64, *95*
Binet, A., 93, *95*
Bolton, N., 66, *97*
Burchard, E.M.L., 63, *96*

C
Cameron, M.B., *98*
Camus, A., 89, *96*
Child, D., 7, *96*, *101*
Christensen, P.R., 52, *97*
Clark, G.A., 91, *96*
Clark, P.M., 40, *96*
Cohen, J., 53, 77, *96*
Cohen, P., 53, 77, *96*
Cooley, W.W., 49, *96*
Costa, P.T., 3, *96*
Cowling, F.G., 86, *101*
Cronbach, L.J., 84, *96*
Cropley, A.J., 7, *96*
Crutchfield, R.S., 86, *96*
Csikszentmihalyi, M., 1, 9, 10, 13, 15, 27, 32, 64, 78, *96*, *97*

D
Davidson, J.E., 30, 86, *96*, *101*
Davis, G.A., 10, 16, 17, *96*, *100*

Day, M.D., 91, *96*
Dillon, J.T., 13, *96*
Dunn, M., 7, *100*

E
Einstein, A., 9, *96*
Ennis, R.H., 29, 30, 39, *96*

F
Field, T.W., 7, *96*, *97*
Firestein, R.L., 33, *97*
Fleming, E.E., 81, 82, *100*

G
Gardner, H., 32, *97*
Gardner, M., 39, *97*
Getzels, J.W., 1, 9, 10, 13, 14, 15, 17, 23, 27, 64, 78, 87, *96*, *97*
Glass, A.L., 32, *97*
Glass, G.V., 84, *97*
Goodman, N., 32, *97*
Gottfredson, G.D., 6, 59, 60, *97*, *98*, *103*, *104*
Gottfredson, L.S., *97*, *104*
Greer, W.D., 91, *96*
Griffiths, A.K., 30, *99*
Guilford, J.P., 6, 13, 35, 52, *97*

H
Haddon, F.A., 7, *97*
Halberstadt, N., 31, *101*
Hanesian, H., 32, *95*
Hansen, J.C., 50, *97*
Hargreaves, D.J., 66, *97*
Harrington, D.M., 6, 33, 34, *95*, *97*
Hattie, J.A., 14, 33, *97*, *98*
Henri, V., 93, *95*
Henry, W., 64, 84, *98*

117

AUTHOR INDEX

Heyde, M.B., 37, 49, *98*
Hocevar, D., 53, *98*
Holland, J.L., 2, 3, 6, 41, 50, 59, 60, *97, 98*, 103, 104
Holyoak, K.J., 32, *97*
Hudson, L., 6, 7, 33, 46, *98*

I
Infeld, L., 9, *96*
Inhelder, B., 29, 30, 37, *98*

J
Jackson, P.W., 17, 23, 88, *97*
Jausovec, N., 35, *98*
Jordaan, J.P., 37, 49, *98*

K
Kastoor, B., 30, *101*
Kelso, G.I., 6, 59, 60, *98*
Kirkland, J., 7, *98*
Klatsky, R.L., 66, *98*
Kogan, N., 14, 16, 34, 52, *102*
Kuder, G.F., 6, *95*

L
Lamb, R.R., 3, 4, 5, 25, 50, 58, *98*
Land, E.H., 86, *98*
Lerner, R.M., 37, *102*
Lewis, D.J., 52, *97*
Lloyd-Bostock, S.M.A., 8, *98*
Lytton, H., 7, *97*

M
Mackay, C.K., 7, *98*
MacKinnon, D.W., 1, 15, 23, 24, 86, *99*
Macworth, N.H., 30, *99*
Maddi, S.R., 78, 85, 86, *99*
Magnusson, D., 10, *99*
Margulies, A., 92, *99*
Matarazzo, J.D., 9, 10, *99*
McCowan, R.J., 33, *97*
McCrae, R.R., 3, 8, *96, 98*
McHenry, R.E., 24, *98*
Mednick, M.T., 66, *99*
Mednick, S.A., 66, *99*
Meyer, R.E., 27, 30, 33, *99*
Milgram, N.A., 60, *99*
Milgram, R.M., 60, *99*
Mirels, H.L., 40, *96*
Moerdyk, A., 7, *99*
Moore, H., 9, *99*
Moore, M.T., 10, *99*

Moustakas, C., *99*
Murray, H.A., 63, 64, 65, 68, *99*

N
Nabokov, V., 1, *99*
Nagy, P., 30, *99*
Noble, C.E., 66, *99*
Novak, J.D., 32, *95*
Nuttall, D.L., 7, *99*

O
O'Keefe, G., 37, *99*
Okuda, S.M., 25, 52, 82, *100*
Osipow, S.H., 49, *99*
Overstreet, P.L., *101*

P
Pariser, D., 91, *99*
Pascal, C.E., 7, *102*
Paulus, D.H., 29, 30, 39, 58, *96, 100*
Pepinsky, P.N., 89, *100*
Pfotenhauer, V., 92, *100*
Piaget, J., 29, 30, 37, *98*
Poole, M.E., 7, *97*
Povey, R.M., 7, *100*
Prediger, D.J., 3, 4, 5, 7, 25, 50, 58, *100*

R
Reitman, W.R., 27, 28, 32, 35, *100*
Rimm, S., 10, 16, 17, *96, 100*
Roberge, J.J., 30, 58, *100*
Roe, A., 63, 85, 86, *100*
Rosenzweig, S., 81, 82, *100*
Rump, E.E., 7, 8, *100*
Runco, M.A., 23, 25, 40, 52, 60, 82, 86, *95, 100*
Rush, J.C., 92, *100*

S
Santa, J.L., 32, *97*
Schmidt, R.A., 61, *100*
Schwabel, M., 29, *100*
Scott, L.E., 10, 11, 37, *101*
Shouksmith, G.A., 24, *98*
Simpson, E.J., 61, *101*
Singer, D.L., 33, *101*
Smilansky, J., 31, 46, *101*
Smith, R.T., 91, *101*
Smithers, A.G., 7, *96, 101*
Snow, C.P., xiii, *101*
Souriau, P., 9, *101*
Stanley, J.C., 84, *97*

Starkweather, E.K., 86, *101*
Sternberg, R.J., 30, 39, 86, *96*, *101*
Stocco, J.L., 50, *97*
Strong, E.K., 5, *101*
Subotnik, R.F., 31, *101*
Super, D.E., 37, 38, 49, *101*

T
Thurstone, L.L., 6, *101*
Tomkins, S.S., 64, 84, *101*
Torrance, E.P., 6, 34, 52, 66, 86, 89, 91, *101*, *102*
Tyler, L.E., 37, *102*

V
Vondracek, F.W., 37, *102*

W
Wakefield, J.F., 1, 3, 15, 35, 50, 53, 64, 82, *102*
Wallach, M.A., 14, 16, 33, 34, 52, *102*
Wertheimer, M., 30, *102*
Whiton, M.B., 33, *101*
Wilson, R.C., 52, *97*

Y
Ycas, M.A., 7, *102*

Subject Index

A

Achievement (school), 23, 30, 46
ACT Interest Inventory, 3–5, 17–18, 22, 39, 51
   sex balance, 4
Alienation, 86, 90
Analogical reasoning, 35
Aptitude tests, 6, 60
Art criticism, 64
Artists, 1, 9, 37, 63–64, 89–90
   artistic problems, 1
   and problem finding, 9
   and society, 89–90
Arts education, 90–93
   and convergent thinking, 90–91
   Discipline Based Art Education (DBAE), 91–92
Arts interest, 5, 49, 58–59
Arts orientation, 2–5, 7–8, 11, 20, 22, 24–25, 45, 60–61, 70, 103–104
   and artistic competence, 20, 22, 25
   employment opportunity, 103–104
   esthetic values, 2, 4
   and problem finding, 60
   and TAT blank card, 70
Arts students, 9–11, 37, 70, 73–75, 78–79, 105–110
   career planning, 37
   divergent thinking, 10
   esthetic values, 9, 11
   imaginativeness, 9
   intelligence, 9–11
   and problem finding, 79
   and TAT blank card, 75, 78
Arts-oriented students, 46–48, 50, 60–61;
   see also Divergers

Arts-oriented students (cont.)
   achievement, 46–47
   creative thinking, 60
   divergent thinking, 46
   insight, 60
   intelligence, 48
   logic, 60
Automaticity, 61

B

Beat Generation, 86
Blank card, *see* Problem finding; *Thematic Apperception Test*
Brainstorming, 92
Business operations (interest), 45, 58;
   see also Well-defined problems

C

California Achievement Tests (CAT), 16
Canonical correlation, 53
Cognitive bias, *see* Converger; Diverger
Cognitive development, 30, 37; *see also* Logic, development
Cognitive skills tests, *see* Creative thinking; Divergent thinking; Insight; Logic
Composing, 31–32
Conformity, 86–90
"Consensual assessment technique," 23
Convergent thinking, 6, 29, 43, 52; *see also* Intelligence; Logic
Converger, 6–7, 33, 45
Creative Behavior Inventory (CBI), 53
Creative behaviors, 3, 53, 58, 60–61
   and cognitive skills, 60
Creative giftedness, 76–77, 79

121

122 SUBJECT INDEX

Creative thinking, xiii–xv, 13–14, 22, 26, 32, 35, 40–42, 46–47, 52, 58–59, 62, 77–78, 81–85, 89–93
  and academic curriculum, 92
  and creative arts programs, 91
  definition, 13
  difficulty, 84–85
  and divergent thinking, 26, 62
  and expression, 32
  by field of study, 78
  and logic, 47, 58, 62, 91
  positively skewed distribution, 77, 81, 83–84
  and problem finding, 26, 62
  studies of, xiii–xv, 22
  tests of, 40–42, 46–47, 82–83
Creativity, xiii–xv, 2–3, 23, 93
Critical thinking, *see* Logic

D

Dead Poets' Society (film), 86
Deduction, *see* Logic
Divergent thinking, 6–8, 10, 24, 33–34, 40, 42, 52, 59; *see also* Pattern and Line Meanings; Unusual Uses
  and arts interest, 8
  and expression, 33–34
  and intelligence, 6–8
  and problem finding, 34
  tests of, 10, 40, 42, 52
Diverger, 6–7, 33, 46
Drawings, ratings of, 9, 17, 22

E

Economy, *see* Meaningfulness
Economy index, 66, 77
Education, *see* Arts education
Emotions, 35; *see also* Expression
Esthetic values, *see* Arts orientation; Arts students
Evaluation, 29, 34–35, 90
Expression, 21, 32–34, 36, 85, 91–92
  emotions, 32–34
  and empathy, 92
  by metaphor, 32, 36
  and transfer, 36

F

Fine arts, 78
Freedom, 85–86

G

Giftedness, *see* Creative giftedness

Group Inventory for Finding Creative Talent (GIFT), 16

H

Hexagon (of interests), 3

I

Ill-defined problems, 31, 34–35
Imagination, 3, 9, 24, 31, 63–64, 77, 84–85, 93
Information processing, 27, 30
Insight, 30–31, 35, 39–43, 46, 52
  and creative thinking, 31
  and divergent thinking, 31
  and logic, 31, 46
  and mathematics, 43
  and problem finding, 31, 46
  tests of, 39–40, 41–42, 52
Intelligence, 5–6, 8, 15–16, 23, 30, 48; *see also* Otis-Lennon School Ability Test; School ability; WISC-R
  and the threshold hypothesis, 15
  tests of, 23, 30
Intuitive perception, 15, 23, 92
  and divergent thinking, 23
  and problem finding, 23
  vs. sense perception, 15

L

Liberal arts and sciences, 78
Logic, 1, 29–30, 39, 41–42, 46, 52, 58–59, 62, 91; *see also* Convergent thinking
  class, 29
  conditional, 29
  development of, 29–30, 58
  and problem finding, 1
  tests of, 39, 41–42, 52

M

Many interests, 3, 24
Meaningfulness, 32, 34, 36, 66, 69, 78; *see also* Economy index
Multiple correlation, 53

N

NEO Personality Inventory, 3
Normal distribution, 82

O

"Open" conditions (on tests), 24, 31, 85; *see also* Ill-defined problems
Openness (to experience), 3, 24

Originality, 3, 22, 76–77; *see also* Problem finding
Otis-Lennon School Ability Test, 39

P
Pattern and Line Meanings (tests), 16
Permissiveness, 86
Positive skew, 84; *see also* Creative thinking
Problem finding, 9–10, 13–15, 23, 30–31, 34, 61, 78–79; *see also* Creative thinking; Insight
  and achievement, 23
  in art, 9
  and blank card, 14–15
  and divergent thinking, 31, 34
  and esthetic values, 9–10
  and originality, 9–10, 30
  prelogical, 14
  in science, 9, 30
Problem solving, 13–14, 26–28, 35
  constraints, 13–14, 27, 35
  prelogical, 14

R
Reasoning, *see* Logic
Remote Associates Test (RAT), 66
Repleteness, *see* Meaningfulness

S
School ability, 46; *see also* Intelligence
Science interest, 5, 49
Science students, 26, 70, 73
Scientific achievements, 60
Scientific orientation, 7–8
Scientifically inclined student, *see* Converger
Scientists, 5, 30
Self-Directed Search (SDS), 3–4, 59, 104
Stanford Achievement Test (SAT), 39
Stereotypes, 88

T
Thematic Apperception Test (TAT), 32, 63–68, 77–78, 83–84
  blank card, 32, 63–64, 66–68, 78, 84
  and creative thinking, 78
  and originality, 68
  and verbal ability, 64, 78
Torrance Tests of Creative Thinking (TTCT), 66
"Tutored images," 92
The Two Cultures (book), preface

U
UNIACT, *see* ACT Interest Inventory
Unusual Uses (test), 52, 66

V
Verbal bias, 8, 24–25
Vocational development, 49
Vocational interests, 5, 38, 103–104
  and intelligence, 5
Vocational Interests of Men and Women (book), 5

W
Well-defined problems, 28–29, 35, 43, 45
WISC-R (test), 16
Writer's block, 23